PRAY OR PERISH

PRAYER POWER SERIES
BOOK 27

ZACHARIAS TANEE FOMUM

Copyright © 1999 by Zacharias Tanee Fomum
All rights reserved.

No part of this book may be reproduced in any form or by any electronic or mechanical means, including information storage and retrieval systems, without written permission from the author, except for the use of brief quotations in a book review.

Except otherwise stated, all Bible references are from the New International Version of the Bible

Published by

books4revival.com

A division of the Book Ministry of Christian Missionary Fellowship International

info@books4revival.com

CONTENTS

Foreword	v
1. Prayer and the Great Commission	1
2. The Critical Importance of Prayer	11
3. Prayer and the Pathway of the Cross	27
4. Prayer and Spiritual Leadership	31
5. Prayer and the Call of God	37
6. Prayer and Fasting Intercession for a Nation	47
7. Prayer Houses	53
8. Prayer and the Self Life	61
9. Prayer and Spiritual Dryness	63
10. Prayer and Accountability	75
11. The Prayer Life of the Lord Jesus	79
12. Prayer and Disharmonious Marriages	85
13. Prayer and Holiness	93
14. Prayer and Lovers	101
15. Prayer and the Raising of Workers	105
16. The Priority in Prayer	109
Back Matters	115

FOREWORD

Prayer is a topic that has been discussed in numerous books, but few have addressed it with the passion and conviction as Zacharias Tanee Fomum did in *Pray or Perish*. As you read through the pages of this book, you will be drawn into the heart of a man who had a deep and abiding love for prayer. Brother Zach, as he was affectionately called, was an authority on prayer and an exemplary prayer warrior.

Pray or Perish is the compilation of his teaching at the Kampala Prayer Conference in 1999, where he emphasized the importance of prayer and how it is crucial to fulfilling God's purpose for our lives. In this book, he makes the point that prayer is not an option but a necessity. He asserts that our very existence in this world is not by chance but by God's definite decision, and we are here to fulfill His purpose. This purpose can only be achieved through prayer, and without prayer, we will perish.

The book is divided into sixteen chapters, each one delving into different aspects of prayer. Brother Zach covers topics such as prayer and spiritual leadership, prayer and the call of

God, prayer and holiness, and many others. His approach to prayer is practical, and he provides insights into how we can develop a meaningful and effective prayer life.

This book is not just theory; it is the fruit of a life wholly given to prayer. Brother Zach's passion for prayer is evident in every chapter, and his deep understanding of the power of prayer comes through in his writing. As you read *Pray or Perish*, we trust that you will be inspired to pray fervently and wholeheartedly, knowing that your life and ministry depend on it.

In addition to his teaching at the Kampala Prayer Conference, this book also contains brother Zach's sharing with the Intercessors for Uganda from his wealth of experience as the leader of the movement of Fasting Intercessors for Cameroon.

We send this book out with prayer that as you read it, you would learn and effectively give yourself to pray so that God's purposes for your life and ministry would come to pass.

1
PRAYER AND THE GREAT COMMISSION

*S*erving in the great commission is a great privilege. Serving God is the highest privilege that mortals can have.

Anyone who wants to serve begs to serve. If you do not beg to serve, you have no place in His service. If anyone is allowed to serve the Lord, the person has been promoted. The service of the King is the highest office on planet Earth.

We beg to serve Him. We are honoured. It is a tremendous promotion. Nothing else is so high.

> *Pray that our eyes would be opened to see that to do anything for God is the greatest honour.*

The one who appoints determines every office. If a chicken appoints you, you cannot be bigger than a chicken. Beg God to give you the privilege of having some place in His service; otherwise you are just a servant of men. The president can only honour you with what he has and as long as he lives. The King of heaven honours you with what He has and as long as

He lives. The King of heaven honours you eternally because He is eternal. There is no change of government in heaven, no elections, no coup d'état. A call to serve the Lord is the most guaranteed employment. I am called to preach the gospel. I practise Chemistry in order to pay the expenses and to have a platform through which to reach the people in the university.

What is your goal in life?

I have experienced the sadness of seeing people wasting their lives.

A man gets to fifty years and you ask him. What have you accomplished in life? He does not know. Worse still he does not know how to spend the next fifty years. Where did he waste the energy of his youth; the dynamism of life? He invested it going around in circles. He lives like a goat looking for food and reproducing. There must be a mission.

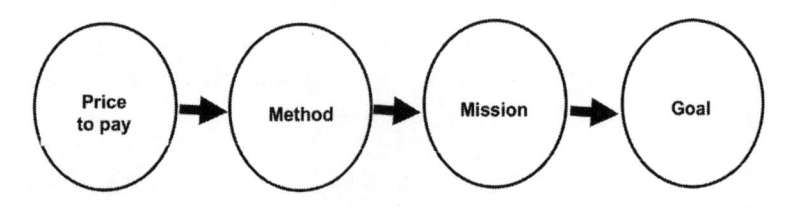

Price to pay → Method → Mission → Goal

God gave us 120 years. We should plan and use it.

Then the Lord said,

> *My Spirit will not contend with man forever, for he is mortal; his days will be a hundred and twenty years* (Genesis 6:3).

The opposite of this is—

> *You sweep men away in the sleep of death; they are like the new grass of the morning—though in the morning it springs up new, by evening it is dry and withered. We are consumed by your anger and terrified by your indignation. You have set our iniquities before you, our secret sins in the light of your presence. All our days pass away under your wrath; we finish our years with a moan. The length of our days is seventy years—or eighty, if we have the strength; yet their span is but trouble and sorrow, for they quickly pass, and we fly away* (Psalm 90:5-10).

God looks at us to bestow His favour.

Confess:

> "I am the object of God's favour."
> "I am the object of God's special favour."

David lived seventy years. After David, Jehoiada lived 130 years.

> *Now Jehoiada was old and full of years, and he died at the age of a hundred and thirty* (2 Chronicle 24:15).

THE POWER OF CONFESSIONS

Be very careful with what you say.

> *... I will do to you the very things I heard you say* (Numbers 14:28).

A people whose speech is full of the word 'death' soon dies off.

> Pray that believers would be very careful with what they say.

Your confession produces what you have. You have the husband that your lips have produced. You have the wife that your lips have produced. You have the economy that your lips have produced. You have the neighbours that your lips have produced.

There is a need to watch over the lips because they are prophetic in their utterance. You are to confess what God wants you to confess before you see.

Abraham and Sarah had to confess what God said and not the evidence of their bodies or circumstances.

> *No longer will you be called Abram; your name will be Abraham, for I have made you a father of many nations. I will make you very fruitful; I will make nations of you, and kings will come from you. I will establish my covenant as an everlasting covenant between me and you and your descendants after you for the generations to come, to be your God and the God of your descendants after you. The whole land of Canaan, where you are now an alien, I will give as an everlasting possession to you and your descendants after you; and I will be their God." Then God said to Abraham, "As for you, you must keep my covenant, you and your descendants after you for the generations to come"* (Genesis 17:5-9).

> *God also said to Abraham, "As for Sarai your wife, you are no longer to call her Sarai; her name will be Sarah. I will bless her and will surely give you a son by her. I will bless her so that she will be the mother of nations; kings of peoples will come from her"* (Genesis 17:15-16).

They were called not to walk according to analysis or what people said. When God says it, it is settled. You risk everything on what God said. There is the testimony of the man healed of goitre who confessed his healing for three months before it became visible. The Bible gives us a similar testimony in John 4:50,

> Jesus replied, "You may go. Your son will live." <u>The man took Jesus at his word and departed.</u>

Faith is taking Jesus at His word and acting on it. When you face a situation, the only question is, "Is there a word from Jesus?" If there is, take that word and act on it regardless of the circumstances. Confess what Jesus has said, Take Jesus at His word.

LIVING FOR THE MISSION WITH A CLEAR GOAL

You are not in this world by accident; I am in this world by God's definite decision. God has a mission for me — a mission that I must accomplish. You are not a goat or a chicken. You were created in God's image to accomplish a mission.

> Then Jesus came to them and said, "All authority in heaven and on earth has been given to me. Therefore go and make disciples of all nations, baptizing them in the name of the Father and of the Son and of the Holy Spirit, and teaching them to obey everything I have commanded you. And surely I am with you always, to the very end of the age" (Matthew 28:19-20).

The mission, "Go and make disciples of all nations," is not a mission God has left for us to start. God has given us a mission. My mission is to go and make disciples of all nations, and to teach disciples to obey all that Christ has commanded. If your mission does not fall within that mission, then it is dangerous. From that mission, you now receive your goal from God; how many disciples you are to make, where and when. Goals are exact, with time limits and can be measured. For example, Go and make 10,000 disciples, in fifty years in a certain country or region.

The mission is one but the goals are different. After the goal has been clarified, you now settle on the method, and the price to be paid. If you don't believe God that you are able to accomplish His mission, you will be put aside. You lay hold on God, then you move forward.

You may need to answer these questions for yourself:

- How many disciples have you made so far?
- How many will you make this year to add to that number?

Jesus made 120 disciples: Those who were at the upper room —the twelve, the seventy-two and the women. But He preached to crowds. His whole ministry depended upon these 120.

Disciples are people you build up to maturity, people on whom the future depends; people whom you teach to obey, not just to feed them with facts. You teach them to obey by your personal obedience.

You cannot build up people without commanding them. A disciple must be commanded to obey; and when he stops obeying, he is no longer a disciple. You don't give him options. You teach him the imperatives of God.

As a disciple, is there a command you are actively disobeying?

Do you know what Jesus has commanded?

Who is teaching you to obey?

Spiritual progress is not accidental. Why are some people more advanced than others spiritually? All of your being must be set out in order to redeem time. Everything must be done to redeem time; you must wage a personal war against indulgence and indiscipline.

The problem with the Pharisees was that they did not obey the word. The leader is not the one who knows more but the one who obeys. The leader is the one who is ahead in obeying the word.

A man who knows five things and obeys all is better than the man who knows twenty and obeys two. It is not how much of the word we know but how much of the word we obey.

In order to make spiritual progress, revelation is a must. Many people know that sin is bad, yet they continue to sin. It is revelation that leads to obedience and until a man has obeyed, his knowledge is useless. The purpose of *Daily Dynamic Encounters with God* is to have what to obey that day. In prayer, you ask God for the power to obey what you learned.

Why do many people not have disciples?

For those who have disciples, how many of them are abiding?

It is because people have fellowship and call it the making of disciples.

The making of disciples is the provision of a model that people copy. It is not by talking. A man sees obedience in your life and then he imitates you.

Disciple making can be illustrated thus:

A man reads the word, the light of God dawns in his heart

↓

He obeys it

↓

He teaches another person to obey even as he has obeyed.

It is a waste of time if you just feed people with facts which is not backed by the example of your life.

The intern has one purpose—to ensure that he would one day do as the professor is doing.

Disciple making is teaching the disciples to obey and the teacher will be judged severely for speaking. Truth is for obeying. It is not just facts exchanged. The devil can steal truth that is in the head. After a truth has been obeyed, the devil is knocked out. To teach advanced theories that excite the teacher, but that is beyond obedience of the people is to commit evil.

Ask yourself, what have I communicated that the people must obey? If they can obey immediately the better.

When you read the word of God, the purpose is to seek what to obey. You only move forward when you have obeyed. God does not want people whose heads are fat with knowledge or fat with ideas.

Disobedience leads to backsliding. You are not in the same position after each disobedience. Every disobedience, however small, pushes a man away from the presence of God. Knowledge that is not translated into obedience separates man from the presence of God.

In a church, how many people are obeying? What are they obeying? To make spiritual progress you should know what God wants and obey it.

To know God's word, you must be a hearer of the word. After you have heard, you can make progress by obeying, or backslide by disobeying.

Everything in the Christian life is tied to obedience.

As you obey, you walk with God.

As you obey you move forward.

As you disobey, you move backwards.

When God speaks to you, you immediately stand at a crossroads—crossroads for promotions or demotions. You are never the same after you have heard God's word. Sometimes, He tells you something very unpopular and you wish you had not heard, but you have heard!

Authority comes from obedience. You cannot lead people to do what you have not obeyed. You cannot teach what you do not practise.

THE CRITICAL IMPORTANCE OF PRAYER

*A*lways jot down what you want to pray about, before you start praying. Do not start praying before you come to terms with what you want to pray about.

Prayer is a must! Pray or perish.

If you don't pray at all, you are nothing.

If you pray very little, you are a very small person, with a small ministry.

If you pray averagely, you are a very small person, with an average ministry.

If you pray extensively, you are a very extensive person before God; so is your ministry. A man is just as great as his prayer life is.

How can we know how important prayer is?

Look at the life of Jesus Christ—the Son of God who came to earth, was prayer important to Him? Was it a priority or something of tertiary importance? What did He practise with regard to prayer?

At twelve, prayer as a must was stamped on His life—as the first must of His life. He was saying to His parents, "Why did you waste three days looking for me? You ought to know that the one place to find Me is My Father's house."

> *These I will bring to my holy mountain and give them joy in my house of prayer. Their burnt offerings and sacrifices will be accepted on my altar; for my house will be called a house of prayer for all nations* (Isaiah 56:7).

There are two aspects of the house of prayer:

The inward house of prayer—the heart of the believer. In the heart of the believer where the Holy Spirit resides, one of His main functions is to take the desires and needs of God, and imprint them on the heart of a believer so that the believer can have God's burden, and can pray God's burden back to Him. It is critical that the human spirit and the Holy Spirit should know oneness for total communication, and total union. If there is total union, the believer can receive the total will of God so that in prayer, he prays back to God the total will of God.

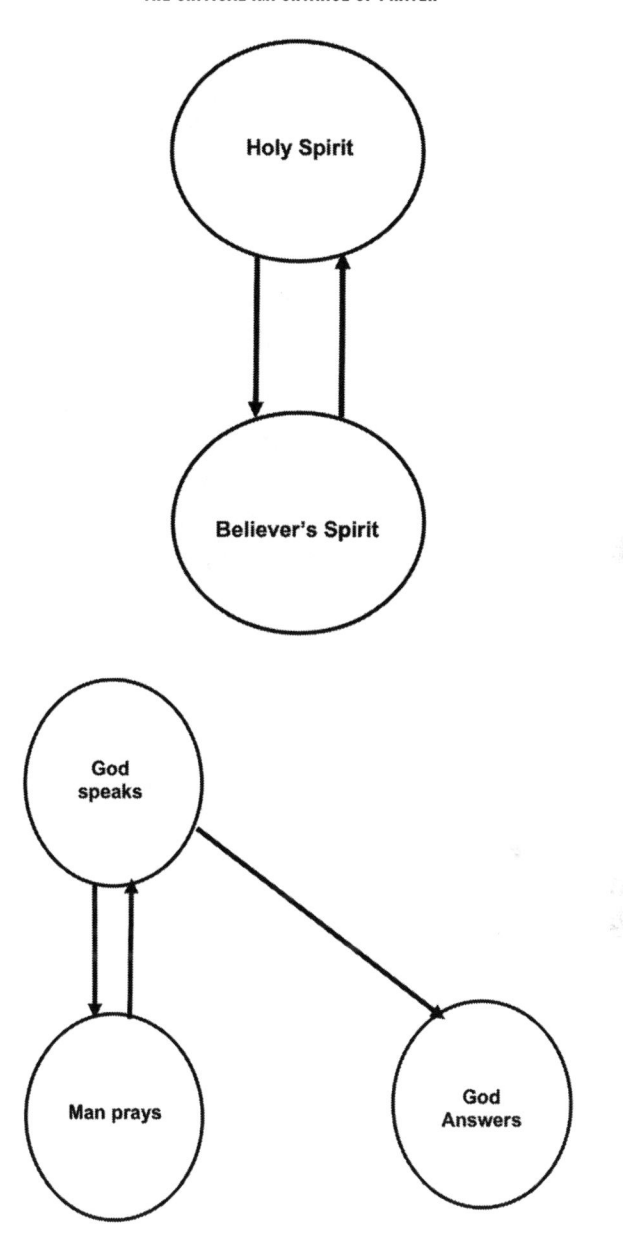

```
        Holy Spirit
           ↕
     Believer's Spirit


   God
  speaks
    ↕         ↘
 Man prays    God
              Answers
```

Prayer begins in the heart of God. As a believer receives what is in the heart of God, he can pray it back to God, and God answers.

It is of critical importance that a believer receives all that God has to give so that he can pray all of it through and receive a total answer.

The first problem is that part of the burden is lost at reception. If God has 100 things on His heart, and if the believer is in a position to receive only 60% then 40% is blocked. If again he only prays back 30%, then it is sad that man can limit God so much. God does not communicate with the mind but with the spirit. Total union is necessary for all to be received. God does not look at the external. His eyes are fixed on the heart. When the first sin comes in, the Holy Spirit can no longer touch the human spirit. The next sin makes the gap wider. Such a person can sing, dance, babble, or preach, but he is out of touch with God. Any preaching outside communion with God is dangerous preaching. The fiercest judgement of God is reserved for those who preach the gospel while they are out of touch with God. Any preaching outside communion with God is dangerous preaching. Whom are you fooling?

You are only fooling yourself because God cannot be mocked. When communion with God ceases, ministry ends and the ministry of death begins.

When a man is out of communion with his wife, he may not stand up and preach at all. If he does, he intends to kill the people of God. If you have no fellowship with your wife, don't go to pray. You will not be praying; you will be making noise.

We are so deceived that we think that we can be in touch with heaven when our

relationships here on earth are broken. It is deception. In Uganda, the older people walked in intimacy with God through a ruthless removal of sin. Sin was dealt with radically and harshly. Generally speaking, the Pentecostals need to go back to the older brethren to learn holiness.

Power without purity should be held in suspicion. Spiritual gifts without holiness should be appreciated with caution.

It is as if the days of Samson are here. After a night with a prostitute, he still lifted the city gate and carried it away. Normally, it should be purity before power. Power with an impure vessel is temporary and will soon pass away. It is not purity without power. It is not power without purity. It is power with the purity of God.

If there is one sin hidden somewhere in your heart that the Holy Spirit has pointed out, and you have not repented of it, then know that you are not in communion with God. Many people ignore sins in their thoughts. They think they are not important.

Blessed are the pure in heart for they will see God (Matthew 5:8).

Those with impure hearts will not see God. Is your heart pure or are you deceived? Are you a hypocrite? The older brethren confessed their sins and forsook them radically.

Dr Joe Church on the secret of an intimate walk with God says, "If you want to make progress, always confess your sins very specifically to God and to man." Call your sins by name —in details, one after another. In Pentecostal circles, either sins are not confessed or they are confessed superficially. They say, "Lord us our sins." You and who?

Africa as a continent has a problem. I am fully convinced that the problem is not political leadership. The church is standing in the way of God. We think that political leaders should improve, but it is the leadership of the church that should improve. The fear of God must return to the leadership of the church.

Hatred of sin must return to the leadership of the church.

Deliverance from the love of money must return.

Deliverance from the love of the things of the world must return to the leadership of the church.

Are you a greedy young minister?

You have an eye on a big car, and you are planning to extort the money from the poor members of the church, and call it "God's blessings," blessings from that God who blesses only the pastor?

Sin separates from God!

I cannot have a revelation of what is on God's heart

I must confront the gap between God and myself.

I must acknowledge the sin that is standing on the way.

> *Do not love the world or anything in the world. If anyone loves the world, the love of the Father is not in him. For everything in the world—the cravings of sinful man, the lust of his eyes and the boasting of what he has and does—comes not from the Father but from the world. The world and its desires pass away, but the man who does the will of God lives forever* (1 John 2:15-17).

We are a generation of lovers of the world and the things of the world. The devil has deceived us that it is prosperity; No it is greed! No man should use the Bible as a tool for swindling the poor.

How do you know a man whom God has prospered?

You know him by what he has given to the gospel, not what he has kept. You may be a young man and God is calling you to serve Him. Don't be deceived by those you see on the pulpits. The first element of prosperity is a heart that fears God.

If you are rich in

- seeking God,
- finding God,
- knowing God,
- loving God,
- hating sin,
- faithfulness,
- integrity,

then you are rich. These are critical elements of prosperity. If you are rich in these, then you are rich indeed. Count your wealth in what you have invested in others; not in what you have kept. Jesus will not share the throne of your heart. If He is to be on the throne, nothing else should be there. He is Lord and King. When He comes into your heart, either He is Lord and King, or He is not in there at all.

People have made prayer an instrument of covetousness.

The apostles were the primary leaders in the church, and the Scriptures cannot be broken.

> *For it seems to me that God has put us apostles on display at the end of the procession, like men condemned to die in the arena. We have been made a spectacle to the whole universe, to angels as well as to men. We are fools for Christ, but you are so wise in Christ! We are weak, but you are strong! You are honored, we are dishonored! To*

this very hour we go hungry and thirsty, we are in rags, we are brutally treated, we are homeless. We work hard with our own hands. When we are cursed, we bless; when we are persecuted, we endure it; when we are slandered, we answer kindly. Up to this moment we have become the scum of the earth, the refuse of the world (1 Corinthians 4:9-13).

Is this earthly splendour? Did God prosper Apostle Paul? If yes, then that is His prosperity. You cannot win Christ and win the things of the world. You will have to choose.

If the love of money can cause you to drag the Most Holy Name into the mud because you desire one thing or the other; I don't know what to say to you.

The love of the world and the love of the things of the world, are the believer's fiercest enemies.

Many will not condemn you for the love of the world. Are you dissatisfied with your clothing, housing? If you are, you are sick. You have a spiritual disease. Even if things are tripled for you, you will not be satisfied. The addition of 20,000 CFA Francs to your salary will not satisfy you.

Has Jesus satisfied you? If your contentment is in the future, it will not come at all. Say, "Lord, I am an idolater," name the idol. Receive from the Lord power to hate it. I must take it out of my life. I cannot tell God to take it; He did not bring it there.

Sin is forgiven when it is forsaken. Many people announce their sins to God, and do nothing about them.

Sin is forgiven when it is forsaken. Have you forsaken the sin you confessed?

Have you carried out restitution? Sins in thoughts are confessed to God alone.

You don't want to preach the total gospel for fear that your members will be few. Are you a preacher of popular messages? Do you want to broaden the narrow way?

> *The multitude of your sacrifices—what are they to me? says the LORD. "I have more than enough of burnt offerings, of rams and the fat of fattened animals; I have no pleasure in the blood of bulls and lambs and goats. When you come to appear before me, who has asked this of you, this trampling of my courts?Stop bringing meaningless offerings! Your incense is detestable to me. New Moons, Sabbaths and convocations—I cannot bear your evil assemblies. Your New Moon festivals and your appointed feasts my soul hates. They have become a burden to me; I am weary of bearing them. When you spread out your hands in prayer, I will hide my eyes from you; even if you offer many prayers, I will not listen. Your hands are full of blood; wash and make yourselves clean. <u>Take your evil deeds out of my sight! Stop doing wrong</u>* (Isaiah 1:11-16).

When the last sin is removed then there can be union. From that intimacy, God will speak, you will hear, then you will pray and God will answer.

The sins that you forget are still against you. God cannot prosper a ministry based on corruption.

The normal Christian life is not—sin—confess—sin—confess.

> *But you know that he appeared so that he might take away our sins. And in him is no sin* (1 John 3:5).

He did not come just to cover sin. He came to take away sin.

Then Christ would have had to suffer many times since the creation of the world. But now he has appeared once for all at the end of the ages to do away with sin by the sacrifice of himself. Just as man is destined to die once, and after that to face judgment, so Christ was sacrificed once to take away the sins of many people; and he will appear a second time, not to bear sin, but to bring salvation to those who are waiting for him (Hebrews 9:26).

But now that you have been set free from sin and have become slaves to God, the benefit you reap leads to holiness, and the result is eternal life (Romans 6:22).

You have been set free from sin and have become slaves to righteousness (Romans 6:18).

He who does what is sinful is of the devil, because the devil has been sinning from the beginning. The reason the Son of God appeared was to destroy the devil's work (1 John 3:8).

And He freed us from our sin, so that we should commit no longer commit sin knowingly.

... *"Look, the Lamb of God, who takes away the sin of the world!* (John 1:29b)

After the suffering of his soul, he will see the light of life and be satisfied; by his knowledge my righteous servant will justify many, and <u>he will bear their iniquities.</u> Therefore I will give him a portion among the great, and he will divide the spoils with the strong, because he poured out his life unto death, and was numbered with the transgressors. For <u>he bore the sin of many</u>, and made intercession for the transgressors (Isaiah 53:11–12)

Many receive Jesus as Saviour but do not receive Him as the sanctifier so that He may set them free from the power of sin —so that sin should not reign in their moral bodies.

> *My dear children, I write this to you so that you will not sin. But if anybody does sin, we have one who speaks to the Father in our defense—Jesus Christ, the Righteous One* (John 2:1).

"My dear children, I write this to you so that you will not sin..." —normal.

"... But if anybody does sin ..."—the abnormal.

Jesus does not only cover sin so that the judgement of God will not fall upon us. He came to uproot sin.

About the love of things, you cannot cling to things and say you are separated from them. How can we cling to that which must go away?

Everything looks for a place in the heart. A small thing can separate you from God.

My decision is that nothing will have a place in my heart. Things must come in through one hand, and leave through the other. If you keep them, they will have a place on your heart.

Something has to go, so that new doors may open. The things of the world vie for the heart.

The spiritual leader must be a model in sacrifice. If he is a model in greed, what will the people become?

The leader is blessed so that he may give.

The leader is prospered so that he may give.

The credentials of spiritual leadership are sacrifice and suffering. A man cannot specialize in greed and lead before God.

The Lord Jesus Christ, although He was rich, yet for our sakes He became poor, so that through His poverty we might become rich, 2 Corinthians 8:9.

You are to make all the money you can honestly make; then invest it in the souls of men, so that through your poverty they might become rich in Jesus.

Whatever God gives to you is meant to be used to make others rich by sacrificial investment into the souls of men. The gospel invites us to become poor so as to make others rich.

Anyone who uses the gospel as an instrument for covetousness is desperately wicked. How much have you invested? How much has the gospel cost you? Where is the self-imposed poverty because of the souls of men?

Paul says, "Because of the souls of men, I have lost all things."

Others say, "Because of the gospel, I have amassed much;" yet they want to preach the gospel Paul preached. When a man has set his heart on money, comfort, ease, he has abandoned the narrow way. That is not the way that the Lamb trod. We must get back to the New Testament model—apostolic model. We cannot fill our hearts with the world, and feel that we can pray and move God.

Oh, that there be seekers of God not seekers of things!

Oh, that they would dream of union with God not the acquisition of things!

Pray and say,

> "Lord, You are my sanctifier.
> Take over my heart.
> Take over my whole life.

In the normal Christian life, if you sin, you do so unknowingly.

God will listen to your prayers if you also listen to his commands. God will listen to the person who listens to Him. God will be moved by the person who is moved by Him. God will ignore the person who ignores God's command. Your prayer will be answered to the extent to which you obey.

Communion with God is the portion of the obedient. When I stop obeying, God will stop answering my prayers. God is seeking a people who, when they pray, it will not be possible to say No!

> *Dear friends, if our hearts do not condemn us, we have confidence before God and receive from him anything we ask, because we obey his commands and do what pleases him* (1 John 3:21-22).

Those who obey His commands, and do what pleases Him, will ask from Him, and receive what they ask.

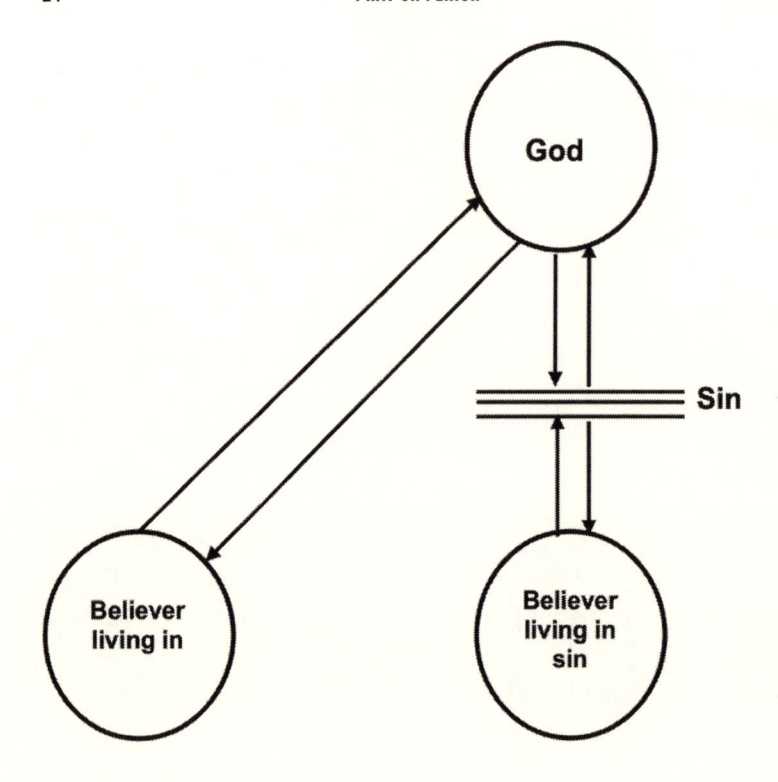

```
        God
         |
         v  ^
    ======|====== Sin
    |     v
Believer    Believer
living in   living in
            sin
```

Sin, known but not confessed and forsaken, ensures that your prayers are not heard, and even the prayers of others on your behalf.

SIN HAS NO DIMENSIONS

A small lie can separate you from God.

Only a fool will joke with sin.

> Pray that you would qualify to pray before you learn about prayer and *t*hat you would be a person to whom God cannot say, "No."

What we see gets into our hearts. You may tell me that you are being civilized by watching television; the sad reality is that you will live to see your children watch all the rot.

3
PRAYER AND THE PATHWAY OF THE CROSS

*A*dopt a lifestyle of voluntary poverty in order that some might be saved who would never have heard the gospel. For fifty years, John Wesley did not increase the amount he lived on. He knew what it meant to tread the narrow way. Self- denial was written in his life, and he succeeded.

Where is that spirit in you?

Where is the ruthlessness?

The heavier the soldier's bag, the less his chances of winning. Sacrifice is a challenge to the believer today. Many have buried the future on the altar of indulgence. Have you ever seen a victorious army trained in indulgence?

Hardship is indispensable for reaching the top.

The pathway that the Lord Jesus trod, the pathway that the early apostles trod, the pathway that all who would make history for the Lord will tread is the narrow pathway.

Where have you sacrificed for the gospel? Where are the marks of self-renunciation because of the gospel in your life? Would you be different by investing the maximum into the perishing souls of men, so that you might alter the eternal destiny of men?

Are you a pastor?

What is your church giving to advance the gospel outside your local church or city? Do you hear the cries of the other nations and close your ears? When your own day of trouble comes no one will hear you.

Somehow there must be rethinking. We must weigh our lives in the light of the perishing souls of men.

Do you want someone to cry, *"am in hell because that sister bought another dress?"*

What has the gospel cost you?

Consecrate your heart so that you will not want what Christ does not want.

Consecrate your ears so that they would not listen to what Jesus would not listen to.

Consecrate your eyes so that they would not give a second look at what Jesus would not look at.

Consecrate your brain so that it would not think of what Jesus would not think.

Consecrate your hands so that they would not touch what Jesus would touch.

Consecrate your feet so that they would not go to where Jesus would not go. They would be obliged to go where Jesus would go and they would go at the speed of Jesus.

You better go or send someone. If you send him, you will let him have what you have, and you will fast and pray to back him.

The Lord Jesus said, *"Go and make disciples of all nations."* The command to go and make disciples was given by Christ to every believer, in every church, in every nation. No nation is too poor. In the USA, lower income women are those who sacrifice to give.

You are personally responsible to the Lord, to make disciples of all nations, beginning from where you are. You are personally responsible for aggressive evangelism. You are personally responsible for aggressive soul winning.

You are personally responsible for aggressive building up of young believers where you are. You are personally responsible for training them, and sending them out to God's worldwide harvest.

There are other parts of this city.

There are other cities of this nation.

There are other tribes of this nation.

The task of bringing the whole world to the feet of the Lord Jesus belongs to the whole church. Your money must go. Your prayer must go. Your fasting must go. All that can be put in must be put in. Your children must be trained to go. All that you can influence must be influenced to go. There must be heavy backing in prayer, fasting and money. There is no substitute for this. If you are not participating in God's worldwide harvest, begin now, and expand as the Lord allows. If not, you may be a spy in the church. Your whole philosophy of life and lifestyle must be rethought in the light of the command to go make disciples of all nations.

If you do not throw away worldly opportunities, how can you get heavenly opportunities?

The missionary enterprise is not an opportunity to go and get the jobs abroad that could not be got at home. One who has not worked and earned money and known how to use money will go for pleasure. It was not jobless people whom Jesus gathered.

Jesus called James and John. Their mother also followed and brought along the purse! There are many excuses for not doing what God wants. The King has commanded. Does it matter what anyone else says?

What will you do with what you have heard?

There is no substitute for prayer. The work before us cannot be done in the power of men.

We cannot go on in the way we have done in the past. Something must happen in the hearts of believers in order to alter the rate, speed and quality of outreach. It must start in your heart and my heart.

New horizons trouble the devil in a new way, enlarge the heart and demand new levels of sacrifice.

4
PRAYER AND SPIRITUAL LEADERSHIP

THE QUALIFICATIONS OF A TRUE LEADER

> *There was a Benjamite, a man of standing, whose name was Kish son of Abiel, the son of Zeror, the son of Becorath, the son of Aphiah of Benjamin. He had a son named Saul, an impressive young man without equal among the Israelites--a head taller than any of the others* (1 Samuel 9:1-2).

The true leader must have no equal. He should be distinctly above the others, because he is to provide a model. He should have far greater spiritual qualifications than others in the following:

- The knowledge of God
- The pursuit of God
- Love for God
- Sacrifice
- Suffering for the Lord and
- *Experience*

They ran and brought him out, and as he stood among the people he was a head taller than any of the others. Samuel said to all the people, "Do you see the man the LORD has chosen? There is no one like him among all the people." Then the people shouted, "Long live the king!" (1 Samuel 10: 23-24).

MAINTAINING LEADERSHIP

Leadership is not automatically maintained. It is determined by who provides the gap. A true leader is a person who, by his spirituality, provides a model for others in his team to follow.

Here is a trustworthy saying: If anyone sets his heart on being an overseer, he desires a noble task. Now the overseer must be above reproach, the husband of but one wife, temperate, self-controlled, respectable, hospitable, able to teach, not given to drunkenness, not violent but gentle, not quarrelsome, not a lover of money. He must manage his own family well and see that his children obey him with proper respect. (If anyone does not know how to manage his own family, how can he take care of God's church?) He must not be a recent convert, or he may become conceited and fall under the same judgment as the devil. He must also have a good reputation with outsiders, so that he will not fall into disgrace and into the devil's trap (1 Timothy 3:1-7).

To desire leadership is honourable. Such a person must also desire to be ahead and work at it, with his eyes fixed on the Lord. The motive of a competitive spirit is self and not the Lord.

Elders are produced at a cost.

Elders are produced at the winepress where the self-life is crushed.

Elders are produced at the cross where indulgence is crucified.

Elders are produced at Jabbok-the place where personal independence is broken.

Elders are produced at all night prayer meetings; the future elders are praying while the non elders are sleeping.

Elders are produced at prayer crusades. Non elders withdraw to sleep.

Elders are produced at prayer sieges. Elders are produced where all is left to follow Christ. Elders are produced where the last trace of sin is abandoned. Elders are produced at Pentecost.

To produce leaders, there first of all has to be a leader. A mediocre person cannot produce leaders. It needs a man who is ahead of others. A leader will seek God, not the post. When a person keeps sin in his heart, he is disqualified. The leader is a workaholic. The leader must be given to long hours of extreme hard work. The leader cannot be indulgent with time.

Leaders are received from God by violent prayer and violent intercession.

Leadership determines the direction the work takes.

How do you know the size of a man's leadership?

In Israel, there were commanders of ten, of fifties, of hundred and of thousands. The number of people that a man leads tells you the impact of his leadership.

How many I am a leader of?

People do not want to answer that question because their self-deception could be exposed.

How do you know those whom you are leading? The people you lead are the people who obey the commands of Jesus as taught by your life and ministry.

Leaders, can you command the people to obey? If they do not obey, what can you do?

Who will correct what they mistook? Who will explain to them what they did not understand?

A leader must not get mixed up. He must ask, "What is my goal?" And keep to his goal. He has to be careful because what is incidental may soon become primary. To succeed in leadership, ask, "Will this activity help me to accomplish my goal?"

Therefore, every day, look at it, and commit yourself to it afresh. A leader must be goal-oriented. It is something about which there must be a definite war.

What is my goal?

120 years x 24 hrs is what you have to do all that God wants you to do to accomplish your goal. Anytime given elsewhere is lost. Give 100% of your time to the people you are leading.

One thing that the enemy does not want is distinctiveness. The enemy cannot stand distinctiveness. If you are just a part of the crowd, then there is no reason being there.

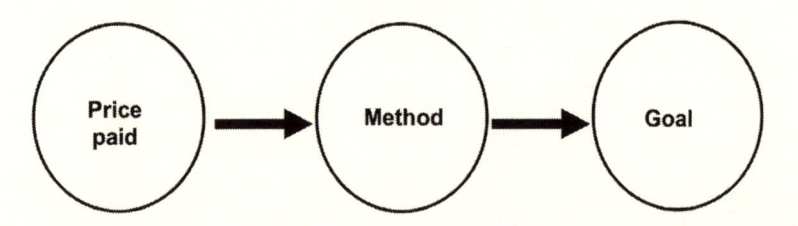

Price paid → Method → Goal

When you have lost the goal, you start looking just at activities.

There is no evaluation—what is it producing?

You should always think in terms of disciples birthed and built up.

The disciples you birth and build up and those birthed and built up by your disciples are the people you are leading. At the end of the day, week, month or year, you should be able to say "I birthed this disciple, and I am building him up. Jesus preached to the masses, but only 120 remained—the 12, the 72 and the women. Any expansion in ministry that does not include expansion in the number of people being discipled is a waste of time.

Whom have I built up? Whom am I building up?

If you only help people to build their houses, where is your own house? Secondary things are enemies of primary things.

What is my goal? To help others?

> *My mother's sons were angry with me, and made me take care of the vineyards, my own vineyard, I have neglected* (Song of Songs 1:6).

A leader must keep at his goal. If he does not, he will be rejected.

Don't organise feasting anywhere. It makes the people spend, and it is a waste of time. If a man does not put a knife to his throat about socializing, he will not succeed to keep at his goal. Everything must be sacrificed for the goal.

Goal-directedness!

Goal-directedness!!

Goal-directedness!!!

The leader must be narrow-minded but broad hearted.

5

PRAYER AND THE CALL OF GOD

The LORD had said to Abram, "Leave your country, your people and your father's household and go to the land I will show you. I will make you into a great nation and I will bless you; I will make your name great, and you will be a blessing. I will bless those who bless you, and whoever curses you I will curse; and all peoples on earth will be blessed through you" (Genesis 12:1-3).

*I*t is God to make us into a great nation, not we to make ourselves. I am troubled about the number of people going out in search of greener pastures.

"I will bless those who bless you."

Whom have you blessed so that God may bless you? Whom have you blessed this week, blessed beyond measure?

People specialize in the ministry of cursing. People spend their time cursing the president and his officials and wonder why things are going wrong.

"...I will curse those who curse you."

When you wish someone evil, God will react.

> *So Abram left, as the LORD had told him; <u>and Lot went with him</u>. Abram was seventy-five years old when he set out from Haran* (Genesis 12:4).

It is dangerous to add to the purposes of God that which was not there from the beginning. We have a dangerous capacity to accommodate. God commanded; Abraham obeyed.

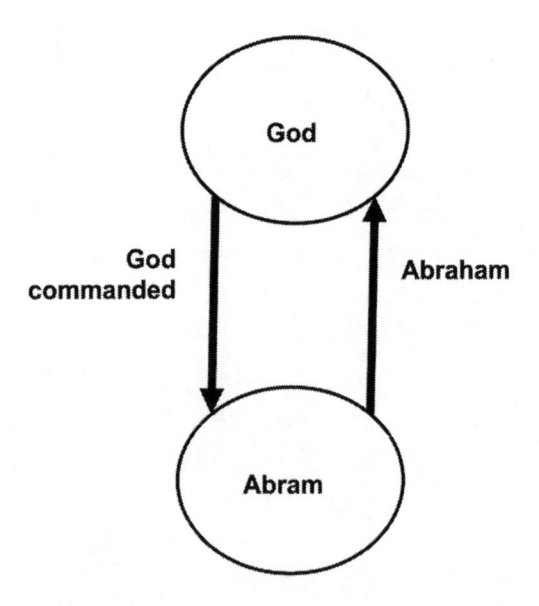

Abram was seventy-five years old when he was called.

Have you ever asked your husband "Where are you taking us to?"

A girl should ask a young man who wants to marry her, "What am I coming to help you accomplish? If people ask that question, there will not be many unhappy marriages.

Many Christian marriages are not happy or they are at best just bearable. The man wanted a cook. Afterwards, he may discover the call of God for his life and find out that the woman was not the right one to help him accomplish it.

No man ought to ask a woman to marry him until he has settled what the call of God on his life is.

Sisters, don't marry a man who has not come to a settled position about the call of God for his life.

The first question a girl should ask her suitor is, "What am I coming to help you accomplish? The second question should be, "Am I the best girl to help him accomplish it?"

Are you married?

Where are you taking your wife to?

When a man is going nowhere, he can be very demanding. He has all the time to invest in going nowhere.

Do you know the call of God on your life?

Is your neck clasped by a collar and your legs in shackles as you go in that one direction?

Is your wife fulfilled?

Does she say, "*I am in the place where God called me?*"

Does your wife say, "*Thank you, my darling husband, for having brought me thus far in God's call?*"

Abraham was called, there was a definite call.

> He took his wife Sarai, his nephew Lot, all the possessions they had accumulated and the people they had acquired in Haran, and they set out for the land of Canaan, and they arrived there (Genesis 12:5).

They set out for the land of Canaan and the arrived there. They got there, then the Lord spoke to Abram:

> *The LORD appeared to Abram and said, <u>"To your offspring I will give this land."</u> So he built an altar there to the LORD, who had appeared to him.*

"To your offspring I will give this land." Abram responded by building an altar to the Lord.

God took the initiative, and Abraham responded with an altar. The Christian life was supposed to be like that—unending intimacy between man and God. God was near. It was a love relationship.

God's priority is not to produce servants of God. What is important is God's will. It is not that which is secure, or without difficulties. God's will is paramount. It is not the call of that which must soon pass away. It is the call of God.

Many brethren at the beginning of their Christian lives do not know anything about the Lordship of Jesus. He comes in as Lord so that He might save us, heal us, deliver us and smash all the curses that keep us in bondage and prosper us.

If you reject His Lordship, you reject Him completely. His Lordship demands that we say, "Yes" to every command of His.

When you say, "Lord," you are saying that your own motives, thoughts, desires shall hence forth be abandoned. When someone says, "Jesus come and be my Saviour but let me do what I want!" Such a person can never be saved.

Abram built a second altar. It was not a response to what God had done. It was an altar of gratitude. Abram took the initiative this time.

The problem with the church is that servants are the ones produced, not lovers. The servant is interested in reward. He is not interested in the master. If a lover comes and has not seen the master, doing the work will be difficult. The problem with our generation is that most people are trained to serve the Lord instead of being trained to love Him so that one day, service would come as an overflow of their love for God.

Pray that the church would return to producing lovers of the Lord.

The love of God has already been poured into our hearts by the Holy Spirit.

And hope does not disappoint us, because God has poured out his love into our hearts by the Holy Spirit, whom he has given us (Romans 5:5).

You don't pour drops. God does not operate a retail shop. He pours out His love.

We are commanded to love, not to ask for love. God's love is in our hearts like water in a huge tank. God says, open the tap to the full; so that the fullness of God's love may flow out. God will not open the tap. Some people open it only a little so that only drops come out. It is a matter of choice. God commands you to open the tap and let the love flow out. He will not open it for you. We are capable of loving. The fullness of it dwells in us, but we will have to choose.

If you are a servant, it is because you have chosen to be a servant—you cannot stand intimacy with Him. If you come there, you will have to take away the things that displease Him. People run away because they want to maintain their dirty self-will, their independence.

Say,

> *"God you've poured Your love in my heart.*
> *God, I have an ocean of love in my heart, love greater than Lake Victoria and it is inexhaustible."*

I have only one heart, the same heart to love the Lord and to love my husband. When you hate one person, you are dead towards all.

I am praying for

- heart expansion for the first year in the new millennium
- unbroken communion with God,
- harmony with my wife.

If you cannot love your wife, you cannot love God. If I close my heart toward one brother, then it is closed. I may think that I am flowing but I am flowing to no one. Praying establishes the word of God. As you establish the word you hear through prayer, your heart is enlarged to contain it.

> *If anyone says, "I love God," yet hates his brother, he is a liar. For anyone who does not love his brother, whom he has seen, cannot love God, whom he has not seen* (1 John 4:20).

For anyone who does not love his brother, whom he has seen, cannot love God whom he has not seen. This shows the hypocrisy of many who say they love God.

> *Can both fresh water and salt water flow from the same spring?* (James 3:11)

The same heart cannot love God and hate man. When there is one person you don't love, you have a heart problem. Don't pretend that you love others. The test case is the people in your house. If we don't love, it is by deliberate choice. Those who love God love people. They forgive those who offend them easily because love is flowing.

Spirituality can be measured by the power to forgive. Those who can keep bitterness for ages have no spirituality.

Is that your problem? God is waiting for you to love the one He has given you, in order to open the way for further revelation.

Why does the church not love God? It is because they are not taught to love men. There are no schools of prayer, fasting, knowing God, walking by faith because there are no teachers. You cannot teach what you do not practise.

The reason why many believers cannot evangelize is that they are empty. The converts do not abide because all they did was a mental exercise. A believer who is half full has nothing to give because he is still desperately in need. A believer who is 90% full still does not have what to give. He is still in need. Even at 99% he still has nothing to give. It is the overflow that goes to others. That is why God pours His love in limitless quantities.

When people come, and we say - preach, preach, preach, they empty themselves out easily and become dry. They don't have anything else to give. If they love the Lord, they will enter into the overflow of love. It is in God's purpose that the believer serves from an overflow of love.

Now there was a famine in the land, and Abram went down to Egypt to live there for a while because the famine was severe. As he was about to enter Egypt, he said to his wife Sarai, "I know what a beautiful woman you are (Genesis 12:10-11).

Abram was in the Promised Land. God was in the Promised Land, and there was famine in the Promised Land. Abram had to say, "I will stay in the promised land."

The question is how could there have been famine when God was there? The famine was there to train Abram in the ways of God.

Difficulties do not necessarily mean that God is absent. The land was the safest place to be, because God was there. But Abram turned his back on God, and went to Egypt because there was famine in the land. Abram left God in the Promised Land, and went away to Egypt.

> *Woe to the obstinate children, declares the LORD, "to those who carry out plans that are not mine, forming an alliance, but not by my Spirit, heaping sin upon sin; who go down to Egypt without consulting me; who look for help to Pharaoh's protection, to Egypt's shade for refuge. But Pharaoh's protection will be to your shame, Egypt's shade will bring you disgrace. Though they have officials in Zoan and their envoys have arrived in Hane* (Isaiah 30: 1-4).

> *Woe to those who go down to Egypt for help, who rely on horses, who trust in the multitude of their chariots and in the great strength of their horsemen, but do not look to the Holy One of Israel, or seek help from the LORD* (Isaiah 31:1)

On his way to Egypt, the man of God became a crook and planned lies for fear of his life. Even though the Canaanites had giants, but with God, Abram was confident because he had God. In Egypt, where there were no giants, Abram became insecure because God was not there.

In Egypt, he lost his wife temporarily. God stopped speaking to him because God does not follow people into their sin. He does not participate in the works of darkness.

> *So Abram went up from Egypt to the Negev, with his wife and everything he had, and Lot went with him. Abram had become very wealthy in livestock and in silver and gold. From the Negev he went from place to place until he came to Bethel, to the place between Bethel and Ai where his tent had been earlier and where he had first built an altar. There Abram called on the name of the LORD.*

He had to come right back to where he had built an altar at the beginning.

Some people say, I will just call on the name of the Lord in Egypt. There is need for harsh repentance, and returning to the place where you first met God.

The hymn writer says:

> Where is the blessedness I knew when I first
>   saw the Lord?
> Where is the soul-refreshing view of Jesus and
>   His word?
> The dearest idol I have known whate'er that
>   idol be
> Help me to tear it from thy throne, and
>   worship only thee.

The dearest idol is yourself. You are your idol. On that altar, you can sacrifice anything.

Abram acquired a lot of wealth in Egypt. Lot acquired a lot of wealth in Egypt.

The wealth served to separate them. It did not serve God's purpose. It did not bless Abraham. Sarai's maid Hagar ended up being the wife of Abraham and this resulted in trouble. Hagar became the mother of Ishmael, from whom comes Islam, the most difficult religion to believe in Christ. There are one billion Moslems on earth today.

He was seeking security but he only brought trouble. For want of a son he yoked himself to a woman who brought the greatest challenge to those who want to win the world for Jesus. What you gather in Egypt in your backsliding will turn bitter ultimately.

6

PRAYER AND FASTING INTERCESSION FOR A NATION

The case of Cameroon

*F*asting Intercession For Cameroon (FIFOCAM) was born in 1977 out of necessity. There was a massive shortage of food.

I asked the Lord, "What should we do?"

We were just starting our Cameroon ministry with a small following.

The Lord told us to set apart Wednesday, for fasting. We obeyed. We were opposed by many Christian leaders. They said we wanted to use the flesh! But we started and God has blessed Cameroon abundantly.

Fasting started in 1978. Right from 1979, the abundance began to flow, until today; there is food in super abundance. Fruits are abundant and of different kinds. God has answered, and continues to answer.

We export food to other countries. God has answered the central issue that led to prayer and fasting. He has answered many others.

- We prayed that the government would have a right attitude to Israel because that is how to tap the blessing of God. Our Moslem president recognized the state of Israel.
- In terms of peace, there are political upheavals all over, but there is peace in Cameroon.
- We imposed peace on the nation.
- We also prayed for a peaceful handover of presidential leadership,

free flow of currency,

new oil deposits being found,

spread of the gospel to other nations,

ease in making passports and others.

In answer to prayer, mountains can be melted. Sometimes we carry out extended fasts when there are special issues.

On the 31st of December 1983, the Lord said to me, "Great plans are being made in hell against your nation, if you care you can stop them. I sent out a letter to mobilize prayer. The result was a failed coup d'état and a failed plan to declare Cameroon an Islamic state. God speaks!

Because God does not speak to everybody, God will speak through one person. If they want to believe him, all will be well and good. If God is to speak to this nation, through whom will He speak? Not everybody will be mobilized, but God's chosen man will be able to mobilize enough people to carry out God's purpose. The problem is with the believers! There are very few who qualify to be intercessors.

Go up and down the streets of Jerusalem, look around and consider, search through her squares. If you can find but one person who deals honestly and seeks the truth, I will forgive this city (Jeremiah 5:1).

If there is falsehood, deceit, hypocrisy and lies in your life and you practise them, then you are eliminated from intercession.

If you are in debt, you cannot be an intercessor for Cameroon because you are dragging the whole nation into debt. I am amazed by the greed that causes people to borrow; it is a way of saying that one has left the narrow way.

A debtor cannot move at the call of God. If you take a loan, and God wants you to leave your job, you cannot leave; you are tied there by the loan. You cannot move. A debtor has placed himself outside the control of the Holy Spirit. He will now be controlled by his debt and not by the Spirit of God.

African nations are in debt here and there. A debtor who is interceding, prophesies debt to that nation. In l984, the Lord spoke to us and said no believer should go into debt.

When a leader goes into debt, he takes all those he is leading into debts. It is a terrible thing to misrepresent a holy office.

There are things that can be done by ordinary soldiers, but the higher up you go, the more authority you have, the more divine backing you receive but also, the more severe the judgements of God. It takes a mad man not to ask, "What will this act do to the call of God on my life?"

By being in debts, you are saying that God will not provide for you, so you will go into the world's system. You have abandoned the narrow pathway and sunk into darkness, especially if you are a leader of intercession. His acts and life are prophetic.

When a man faces difficult times, instead of staying with God in the Promised Land, he goes to the Egypt of borrowing. He has chosen to abandon the narrow way. Do you know when the Lord will call you? Do you know if He will keep you there to pay your debt?

Unless there is a radical difference between the believer's attitude to money and the world's... Are we serving a living God? If a man fails in money matters, he has failed the ultimate test because where your treasure is, there your heart will be also.

> *Do not be afraid, little flock, for your Father has been pleased to give you the kingdom. Sell your possessions and give to the poor. Provide purses for yourselves that will not wear out, a treasure in heaven that will not be exhausted, where no thief comes near and no moth destroys. For where your treasure is, there your heart will be also* (Luke 12:32-34)

When people keep their treasures on earth, their hearts are earth-bound. When their treasure is transferred to heaven, their hearts will become heaven-bound. I will not try to disciple someone whose treasures are on earth because his mind will be on earthly things.

> *"I the LORD do not change. So you, O descendants of Jacob, are not destroyed. Ever since the time of your forefathers you have turned away from my decrees and have not kept them. Return to me, and I will return to you," says the LORD Almighty. But you ask, "How are we to return?" Will a man rob God? Yet you rob me. But you ask, "How do we rob you" "In tithes and offerings. You are under a curse—the whole nation of you—because you are robbing me. Bring the whole tithe into the storehouse, that there may be food in my house. Test me in this," says the LORD Almighty, "and see if I will not throw open the floodgates of heaven and pour out so much blessing that you will not have room enough for it. I will prevent pests from devouring your crops, and the vines in your fields will not cast their fruit," says the LORD Almighty. "Then all the nations will*

call you blessed, for yours will be a delightful land," says the LORD Almighty (Malachi 3:6-12).

God said, "Put me to the test." This is the only incident in the Bible!

On 24 October 1993, I prayed, "I put You to the test O Lord in the matter of giving 83% of our income to the Lord."

While in India on 13 October 1999, I was shocked by the poverty I saw there. As a result, we moved up our giving to 90%. On 27 July …., we moved further to 91%.

A leader prophesies with his money. We have not in any subsequent year repeated the same percentage of the previous one since 1976.

In Ezekiel, the prophet spoke by his actions. God led the prophet to act in the place of Israel. God acts by feeding a prophet by ravens. Know that with the little oil, all the jars could be filled. Know that with a little oil and a little flour, you can be fed over a period of time. If a leader fails in his faith in God with regard to earthly things, how can he lead men?

If God cannot give you basic needs, how can He give you the reaping and preservation of the souls of men? If you withhold what is less than the dust of heaven, how can you handle heavenly wealth? I labour to ensure that there be

- no lie in my life;
- no lie in my finances.

> Confess that God is a God of abundance then the harvest will follow.

7
PRAYER HOUSES

*P*rayer houses are places set aside by man exclusively for prayer. Your house may not be a place where you can really pray especially if you have that great enemy called the telephone because when it rings it disturbs. Thus, you need a place where the phone should not ring.

When a person withdraws to meet God, he should leave the world outside. Why should people be calling him? When a person goes to pray, he should not be disturbed. If you cannot afford a house, there should be rooms.

Our house of prayer in Yaoundé has twelve rooms. But there are other rooms set aside.

We also have the Douala house of prayer for all nations.

Two years ago, the Lord led us into the battle for the overthrow of the satanic prince of Douala. We fasted for fourteen days and did a prayer walk in the city. We walked from east to west 30km; then from north to south. It was conflict but the Lord saw us through.

There must be centres for warfare.

Prayer is warfare. Warfare requires warfare places.

It is disastrous to send missionaries out and not back them with heavy praying.

On the mission field, the missionary should first establish a room for prayer before going to do other things. If he does not, he is a fool. He must find a room from where he will move God. His life will move God. As soon as they start bringing people to God, they recruit these to pray. The place of prayer is where the action is.

Prayer is the most important business on planet Earth.

Prayer is the most difficult business on planet Earth.

May God open your eyes to see that a prayerless work is no work. A man can work after he has prayed. Before he has prayed, there is nothing he can do.

I gave this prescription to missionaries: Spend the time from 4:00 am to 12:00 noon with God. Afterwards go and do the work outside. Unfortunately, they don't obey. That is active co-operation with Satan.

The devil only fears praying men. The devil does not fear talking men and mere preachers. The devil can laugh when you are preaching but when you pray, there are emergency meetings in hell.

The 1990 prayer crusade went on for eight to ten hours each night for 51 nights. We were labouring for sanctification in the ministry. Approximately 120 people participated.

We have full-time people for prayer. They receive an allowance to live on in order to put in eight hours of prayer daily. Such people need two times the salary of a preacher.

I am troubled because when it comes to full-time ministry in prayer, it is mostly women who volunteer.

The number one person in the ministry is the number one person in prayer. Promotion should be by prayer. The last person in the ministry is the last person in prayer.

Prayer is moving God to act. A man's power is measured by the extent to which he can move God to answer prayer.

In heaven, you will not be asked, "What mansion were you living in?" Mansions on earth cannot be compared to toilets in heaven. When a man wants to pray and cannot find a place to pray, he feels like breaking.

Give this city houses of prayer. Let the houses of prayer be your heavenly houses on earth, instead of just enjoying your earthly houses. Every church should set aside places for prayer. This should be obeyed urgently.

Stop socializing. Convert socializing time into prayer time.

> *When all the people were being baptized, Jesus was baptized too. And as he was praying, heaven was opened and the Holy Spirit descended on him in bodily form like a dove. And a voice came from heaven: "You are my Son, whom I love; with you I am well pleased"* (Luke 3:21-22).

Others came, were baptized and they went away, but the Lord Jesus, after He was baptized, converted the banks of River Jordan into a house of prayer. From there He began to storm heaven.

> *Oh, that you would rend the heavens and come down, that the mountains would tremble before you! As when fire sets twigs ablaze and causes water to boil, come down to make your name known to*

your enemies and cause the nations to quake before you! For when you did awesome things that we did not expect, you came down, and the mountains trembled before you (Isaiah 64:1-3).

There are two planes to the heavens:

1. There is that which only God must rend; and God has already rent the heavens.
2. Now man must rend the heavens. The prayers of the Lord Jesus were like ballistic missiles that rent the heavens.

Non-violent praying is no praying at all. You cannot reach heavens unless you know you must have answers or there is trouble.

Before Jesus started to pray, the heavens were sealed. As He started to pray, the heavens remained sealed. The prayers went as swift missiles until they tore open the heavens so that the power of God could come down. The heavens must be rent!

As He was praying, the heavens were rent, because the prayers of the Lord tore open the heavens.

Jesus was born of the Holy Spirit. There was no time He didn't have the Holy Spirit. Had Jesus been baptized and gone away, He would have gone away with an important ministry. When were the heavens opened to you? When did the Holy Spirit come upon you? The problem with the church is that many unanointed ministers use the power of oratory, bible school power or seminary power, but these cannot substitute for the power of the Holy Spirit. Until the anointing has come, nobody has the power to minister anything. Jesus told the disciples to tell no one that He was the Christ.

> *Stay in the city until you have been clothed with power from on high* (Luke 24:49b).

All the naked ministers are not clothed with the power from on high. He was God, yet He needed the anointing; and you? Are you better than Jesus? No! You are dangerous.

The heavens open to praying men and women.

> *The Spirit of the Lord is on me, because he has anointed me to preach good news to the poor* (Luke 4:18a).

The Lord could say, the Spirit of the Lord is upon me, for he has anointed me to preach the Good News to the poor. Anointed to preach the good news! If I know that a man is not anointed, I will not listen to him. What am I listening to? The clever analysis of a clever mind?

To those who are not anointed, the command of Jesus is, "Tell no man." You will fill their heads, not their hearts. It needs the anointing to touch the hearts of men. It was never in God's purpose that those who are not anointed should preach the gospel of the One who was anointed. If one could be exempted from being anointed it would be the Lord Jesus, but He was anointed.

When were you anointed?

> *On one occasion, while he was eating with them, he gave them this command: "Do not leave Jerusalem, but wait for the gift my Father promised, which you have heard me speak about* (Acts 1:4).

The anointing is the divine ability to preach the gospel so that it produces convincing and converting power such that the gospel arrest people and transform them for God.

Some people say they are converted but they lie like devil. Part of the problem is that they are the fruit of powerless preachers who bring people to natural decisions, without the power to transform their hearts.

> *Jesus, full of the Holy Spirit, returned from the Jordan and was led by the Spirit in the desert, where for forty days he was tempted by the devil. He ate nothing during those days, and at the end of them he was hungry* (Luke 4:1-2).

JESUS IN THE WILDERNESS

Mighty anointing came upon Jesus and the Holy Spirit led Him into a forty-day fast.

When the Holy Spirit comes on a person, he should go on a fast. Jesus is the model.

Some say Jesus fasted for all of us; so we should get and eat.

We are a generation that loves food! And every reason is given to run away from fasting. Satanists fasted forty-days to destroy the marriages of Christian leaders. If the devil destroys your marriage, he has destroyed your ministry. It is amazing that one who cannot lead his wife wants to lead the church of 500.

Until the church is weaned from the love of food, there will be very little victory. The church cannot be weaned from the love of food until the pastor carries one critical burden for the continent—spiritual leadership.

You cannot have a pastor who loves money and a congregation which gives sacrificially. Leadership is the call to provide a model!

A pastor who prays intensely will have a church which prays intensely.

A pastor who loves the Lord will bring his people to love the Lord

A worldly pastor will infect his people with the love of the world. When you have chosen your pastor, you have made a very far-reaching choice.

If should ask, "What are you initiating your children into? Into indulgence? Until there is proper leadership for the churches, we cannot see great things happening. Unless there are godly, consecrated pastors, the church will remain carnal. Unless there are godly fathers and mothers, the children will not be introduced into the deep things of God.

What model are you providing for your children?

Are your children growing in a fasting environment? Are they growing in an environment where there is warfare in prayer? What kind of father are you? Your children will become like you. What model are you providing?

If you want to marry a girl, first go and investigate her father. Our fathers were wiser than our stupidity. They investigated the family. The daughter will be like the father.

Investigate the consecration of the parents, their attitude to the laws of God and the nation. If not, you will marry a twenty-five-year-old tree twisted according to the father or mother. To change her will need another twenty-five years.

The model that the parents provide is critical for her future.

You are building the next generation by your fasting, by your prayers ....

What do your children know not to be the priority of your life?

The most critical hours of the day are between 4:00 and 7:00 a.m. What a man does with his time matters a lot.

The maximum fast—forty days. Only the flesh can cause a man to try to beat Jesus in fasting. Forty days is the limit according to the Lord Jesus, Moses, and Elijah.

Generally speaking:

In prayer a man reaches out to God. In fasting he reaches out against the devil.

In praying the Lord Jesus encountered God! In fasting He reached out against the devil.

The Lord Jesus said, "When you fast..." not if you fast!

> *<u>When you fast</u>, do not look somber as the hypocrites do, for they disfigure their faces to show men they are fasting. I tell you the truth, they have received their reward in full. <u>But when you fast</u>, put oil on your head and wash your face* (Matthew 6:16-17).

8

PRAYER AND THE SELF LIFE

One of the greatest enemies of the Christian life is the self-life.

> *I have been crucified with Christ and I no longer live, but Christ lives in me. The life I live in the body, I live by faith in the Son of God, who loved me and gave himself for me* (Galatians 2:20).

That is God's answer to the self-life. I have been crucified with Christ.

The self in me was crucified. I am no longer under the powers of self. Jesus is my Deliverer. I now have the life of Christ. When He died, He included me in His death. I, too, died.

I am dead. The self-life was crucified. The "I" in you was crucified. If I am crucified with Christ, then I am nothing. If you have been crucified with Christ, then the self has been crucified and you don't have to obey it. My self-life died. It was crucified with Christ. I leave it at the cross and I am free.

You need to celebrate the death of self.

As far as self is concerned, I am a corpse.

I see before me just two wills ...

Have you known God's will and you are wondering whether you should obey? Are you in conflict? Are you in turmoil? All of your being is troubled because you know what God has said and you know what obedience would mean, but you will not obey?

There are many people seeking to do many things for God. The secret of the life of Jesus is that He did not invent any programmes. He just obeyed what His Father told Him.

The walk with God stops when obedience stops.

9

PRAYER AND SPIRITUAL DRYNESS

ITS MANIFESTATIONS, CAUSES AND CURE

*A*s I travel, I find that many spiritual leaders are dry. They are not thirsty. They are dry. Thirst or hunger is the property of those who desire food or drink. If a person wants more of the Lord, more of the things of the Lord, he is thirsty.

It is a blessing to find a hungry and a thirsty man. If you give him food, he will be satisfied. A dry person is a tragedy because often such a person was once full. He was enjoying the Lord and serving him out of overflow but he fell into the trap of the devil and he began to give more than what he was receiving. When a man begins to spend more money than he is receiving, then he has a sick soul, until he become dry bones.

My time spent with God daily (on average) in prayer alone or with others, daily dynamic encounters with God, the word, waiting on God is nine hours fifteen minutes. When it drops to eight hours, I begin to tread on dangerous grounds. If a man used to spend eight hours with God then his ministry increases and he is mad enough to reduce time spent with God in order to minister some more, it is real madness; it is the pathway to the grave. It is not ministry. It is spiritual suicide because ministry is the overflow of a man's knowledge of God.

The more overflow, the more ministry. Less overflow, less ministry. No overflow no ministry. But because of the corruption of our generation, people expand the territories and the devil deceives them that they are expanding their ministry. No! Ministry is the overflow of spiritual wealth.

For example, when does a person put on weight? When he eats more food than he can use. In the Old Testament, the Lord said that the fat is for the Lord. The Lord was saying it is the overflow that is unto God. It is the overflow that is ministry. People continue to expand their activities until they are dry. People continue to suck you until you are totally dry.

From the beginning, when he begins to reduce his time with God, it will not be obvious because he is using the fat that was stored in the past. But with time, he gets dry. If a man used to spend eight hours with God and he is invited to do other things, you should know that the eight hours with God is sacred. He needs to take time from sleep or from other activity.

If the person is deceived, seduced and a hypocrite, he will reduce the time with God in order to spend more time with man. Initially, he may seem to be all right because of what was stored in the past. Very soon, these reserves will be exhausted. Ministering in this condition will result in no expansion in ministry, no impartation of life, no revelation communicated.

A church may begin to grow in numbers, but it is growth in numbers of starving people because the minister is not feeding himself. After a time, the man may become a bigger denominational leader receiving more invitations to minister. But that is the man who will soon fall into adultery or fornication, fall in love with the world ....

When the glass was full, there was no place for the love of the world, the love of money, the love of self, debts. The sad thing about people who are dry is that they no longer hunger for God.

Spiritual hunger is the possession of those who are filled with God. Spiritual thirst is for those who are filled with God. The empty do not hunger for God. The dry have lost the power to hunger and to thirst for God. As they get dry, they get less thirsty.

As a man dries up, sin, the love of the world come in, to the extent that he commits sins which even the unbelievers would be ashamed of. He will hate prayer meetings.

He only prefers group praying. When alone, he is short of words after three minutes.

In daily dynamic encounters with God (DDEWG), he only copies some verses and soon he is done.

They may have large crowds but no ministry. They are very sick.

Immediately a person finds that he is spending less time with God than he did in the past, he should stop everything he is doing, and go to seek God. If he continues, he will kill the people because he is ministering death.

Pray that God would plant the word in our

hearts, that we would obey, that hypocrites who stand before men would withdraw.

Dry men can only minister death.

A person could be dry, very dry or very, very dry.

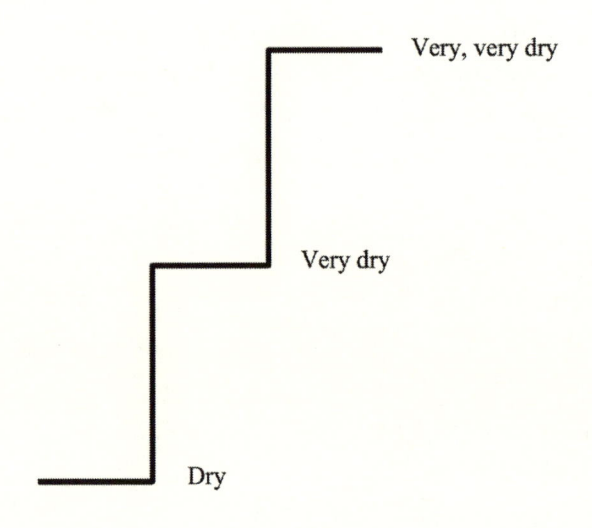

```
                              ──── Very, very dry

              ────── Very dry

 ──── Dry
```

Many people are very dry. They even find God's presence distasteful. When they find a spiritual person, they may want to talk about their spiritual condition but with no desire to change now. With God, they are strangers. In prayer, they utter some ugly noise to God, then they start fidgeting. Their minds start roaming. There is a secret enjoyment of the company of the world, the love of fame. For them those who are walking on the narrow way are exaggerating. It is because of the decay within. In meetings they love superficial singing. They like songs of praise with empty words

One tithing that troubles me is the disappearance of hymn books. When superficiality is the order of the day, hymn books disappear; and superficial songs are sung, after which people go back to sin.

At evangelistic meetings, people are clapping; they are not troubled. The convicting power of God is not there. Words which pierce the heart are not there. It's a big lie when people are told: Come and Jesus will solve your problems, take away your diseases and so on. For some of us, problems began when we believed. There are no problems when you are going down stream, but go against the current and you will drown! That is not the gospel. Jesus says, "Come and take up your cross," come and take on the burden of the cross. Come, forsake the world. God is not in trouble. He cannot be in trouble.

No one can add to or subtract from His stupendous glory.

Even if no one believes! God is beyond human favours. Man comes to God for his own good!

THE CHARACTERISTICS OF DRY PEOPLE

Are you dry, very dry?

One characteristic of dry people is that they move from one church to another in order to escape responsibility and escape obedience. They become testers of preachers instead of letting the word of God test them.

We need more people who suffer stomach ache, because of their sins. If you are walking with God, there are levels:

Gasping and panting
For a long time I have kept silent, I have been quiet and held myself back. But now, like a woman in childbirth, I cry out, I gasp and pant (Isaiah 42:14).

Thirst or panting
As the deer pants for streams of water, so my soul pants for you, O God. My soul thirsts for God, for the living God. When can I go and meet with God? (Psalm 42:1–2).

Hunger
Blessed are those who hunger and thirst for righteousness, for they will be filled (Matthew 5:6).

The Bible says,

Blessed are those who hunger and thirst for righteousness, for they will be filled (Matthew 5:6).

When he was in the Desert of Judah. O God, you are my God, earnestly I seek you; my soul thirsts for you, my body longs for you, in a dry and weary land where there is no water. I have seen you in the sanctuary and beheld your power and your glory.

Because your love is better than life, my lips will glorify you. I will praise you as long as I live, and in your name I will lift up my hands. My soul will be satisfied as with the richest of foods; with singing lips my mouth will praise you. On my bed I remember you; I think of you through the watches of the night. Because you are my help, I sing in the shadow of your wings. My soul clings to you; your right hand upholds me (Psalm 63:1–8).

The Psalmist beheld the Lord; because of his spiritual experiences, all of his being longed for God.

> *I open my mouth and pant, longing for your commands* (Psalms 119:131).

When the hungry are not fed, it leads to dryness. The more a thirsty person drinks, the more he will thirst: his satisfaction creates more thirst for the Lord, so that he is goes higher and higher. If he is thirsty and does not drink of the Lord, the dryness will intensify. When a person is thirsty, it is a good sign. It tells you that he is walking with God. If he is thirsty and does not drink, the dryness will intensify so much that he gets to a place where he abhors God. Even if he is given the wine of the spirit, he will not respond. He is dead.

God had become your dwelling place but you departed from the Lord, and you became a servant of man. involved in more and more activities and having less and less time for God, until cobwebs have grown in the place of prayer!

Your knees are sore such that when you kneel to pray you have to soon stand up.

> *For a long time I have kept silent, I have been quiet and held myself back. But now, like a woman in childbirth, I cry out, I gasp and pant* (Isaiah 42:14).

You hunger for food and you can go for forty days without food.

You thirst for water and normally you can go for seventy-two hours without water. (The purpose of fasting is not to destroy the body)

Gasping is the desire for air in the experiment of breath-holding, most people could not stand thirty seconds. Gasping after God is an experience that very few people have ever experienced. They know the kind of intimacy with God that even

a little time out of contact is shattering and they will come back to God at any cost. They are desperate for God at any cost. The way to gasping is the overflow of the deepest intimacy with God.

It is not just that there is nothing between you and God, when there is fusion, you will know the intimate gasp of totally losing yourself in Another. On the other hand, you will also know when it has weakened. Many believers do not know anything about this, because they do not know jealous intimacy with God.

From personal experience, I once had to return a bow tie I bought in Nigeria to the seller. Another time I had to remove the fan and then a cassette player from my office. Yet on another occasion, I had to return a cheque of $500 before I regained my peace with God.

Are you jealous for the gasp? Are you jealous for the firmness of that gasp or have you something less? God speaks in general when we are far. God touches specific issues when we are near and that is the only way to respond. God speaks specifically so that there may be specific responses. God speaks that there may be obedience at a specific level.

> *My people have committed two sins: They have forsaken me, the spring of living water, and have dug their own cisterns, broken cisterns that cannot hold water* (Jeremiah 2:13).

Do you seek God? Do you read the bible to find God or you read the bible to cover chapters? Do you pray to find God or to cover hours? Is it activity or communion? Do you come and say, "Lord do not let me depart without seeing Your face?" Do you say, "Lord I don't want to analyze Your word?"

I want to meet You? Are you troubled because of His demands?

They have forsaken the Lord. Many churches can go on without God for years. They have set up a system that can go on even if God is out. They are not troubled by the fact that God has not spoken or that the word of God no longer pierces their hearts. They are just going on and on and on.

They have forsaken the Lord. They have dug their own graves. It may even be the routine of praying from 8:00-12:00 without God and having all night meetings where God is absent. Evangelism without passion, telling people about God but not troubled in the heart to the extent that no one believes. Jesus did not say, "Come and I will make you attempting fishers. A fisherman who does not catch fish is out of the job. Does God want evangelism or souls won? The Lord seeks a harvest of souls won. Forsaking the Lord, the cistern of living water, they have created broken cisterns— time spent in evangelism instead of souls won, decisions instead of souls added to the church.

Do you record decisions or people who have been baptized and are in the local church? Soul winning only ends when the person believes, is baptised into water and the Holy Spirit and is in the local church. Then the work of building begins. To count people as belonging before these steps are completed is a waste of time. Dry people have a universal capacity to produce decisions that are not conversions. There may be a moving forward; they may say the sinner's prayer but there is no repentance toward God and no faith in the Lord Jesus.

> *... I remember the devotion of your youth. How as a bride you loved me ...* (Jeremiah 2:2).

SHOCK TREATMENT: THE ANSWER TO SPIRITUAL DRYNESS

Do you remember the devotion of your early days in the Lord? How is it that you have become such a disaster? Before, His presence held you spell-bound, but now you are infatuated with the love of the world, and your soul has gone dry.

Do you not see that now you are a caricature of the person you used to be? Are you not shocked about your own performance? Throw away the broken cistern.

What is the way out of spiritual dryness?

The answer to spiritual dryness is not the return to former things. It will not work. **It is shock treatment!** If you go at a normal pace you will soon give up. For example, going back to ten chapters of the Bible-No, go to forty or fifty chapters. If you were seeking God for one to two days per week, and became dry, go for seven days unceasingly.

If you were praying two hours in a day, go for ten to twelve hours and continue until the hunger returns.

Continue the shock treatment until,

- the hunger returns.
- the hunger is re-established.

When a woman begins to accuse her husband, she soon dies spiritually. Believers who criticize church leadership will dry up.

During the inauguration of the Abuja house of prayer, a sister in Nigeria touched God afresh in the fifteen hours of praying in tongues in twenty-four hours.

Many brethren came to new breakthroughs through the ninety-six-hour prayer siege.

In Uruguay someone read 240 books in six months. This is the shock treatment.

Dryness is a crisis condition. It is a desperate condition. It is next to spiritual death. Normal ways of treating it will not solve the problem. Shock treatment must be undertaken.

PRAYER AND ACCOUNTABILITY

The question of integrity of preachers is a serious matter. In the early 70's, there was a distinction between a man who was employed and a man who was preaching. If you can testify by your own life about what you are saying, you are preaching. To "preach" theories is mere speaking! It will not produce results. It is better not to speak theories than to lead the people of the Lord astray. How can you testify that what you are saying is true? First show people that you give, if you are going to talk about giving money. If you are going to talk on marriage, first prove to them that yours is working. If you are going to talk on the family, first prove that your own is working.

How can you know how much you pray if you are not accountable?

1. Record your prayer time.
2. Prove not only that you spend time in prayer but that God answers prayers. After the prayer crusade in 1990, the Lord asked us to write one thousand prayer

topics and see the extent to which God has answered. This should be on critical issues. Secondly have a routine prayer book.
3. Have Daily Dynamic Encounters with God (DDEWG) with a heart cry that God may speak to you as a person.

My DDEWG is God operating surgery in me and leading me. The record of my battles with God; my wrestling to know Him, waiting on Him and hearing His voice.

If the Director General calls his secretary and she doesn't come with a pen and a notebook, she will soon be out of the job. When we appear before God, it is important for every one of us to come prepared to record what He will say. Sometimes, He gives revelations about the work, the children or revelation of the meaning of a passage.

<u>Growth in DDEWG</u>: I started with thirty to forty-five minutes. Now three to four hours leaves me unsatisfied because of the spiritual science of entering into the presence of God.

If you are dealing with someone who outweighs you utterly, when you get into his presence, you don't start talking like a fool, you wait for him to speak then you plug in. When you come before the Lord, you have just come out of the noisy world. The noise of all that you heard is still ringing in your mind. You have to wait until both the external and internal noises should cease. After this you can now speak. There can now be communion with God.

All that is done in a hurry is superficial.

Here is my prayer book and my book for Daily Dynamic Encounters with God. The purpose of the demonstration is to serve both as a testimony and a challenge.

The relationship with God is a sum total of everything. Not to take it seriously is terrible. If you believe that God is talking to you, how can you just record it anywhere? When you pray and forget what you prayed, how do you expect God to answer? The purpose of writing prayer topics is to enable you to continue praying until God answers. The unanswered prayers tell me that you are still here in battle with God. Get a note book, record your prayers and prove that God answers your prayers. For some prayer topics, don't tell others in order to have personal proof that God answers your own praying.

You may be blocked but the other person may not be blocked. Everybody must have undeniable proof that God answers his/her prayers.

We do not only want to encourage you to pray. Establish prayer records. As someone called to preach and write on prayer, Woe is me if I don't pray!

Advertising for funds? If we cannot move God to give us shillings, Deutschmark, pound sterling, how can we move Him to transform character?

We don't want artificial expansion. The ministry grows as our hearts expand to know God more. If you cannot move God through prayers and you believe in manipulating man, you are shallow!

The leader is called to provide a model. Leadership is the call to provide a model. The leader must say, Be ye imitators of me as I am of Christ. If not, he has no mandate for leadership. If you are already a leader, provide a model in prayer.

How do you plan the future?

First set aside time for prayer and fasting. Then other things can fit in. I will take a ten-day shut-in retreat in December, fasting from seeing man, talking to man, being talked to by man, so as to hear God and talk to Him! Next year it will be fourteen days.

The rest of the days can be used for travelling and ministering.

You cannot leave the future to chance and expect to provide leadership. What is not planned and prayed for may never be. Pray to bring into total maturity all that we are and all that we have in the pursuit of God; and to make sure that there are models for the younger generation.

11

THE PRAYER LIFE OF THE LORD JESUS

That evening after sunset the people brought to Jesus all the sick and demon-possessed. The whole town gathered at the door, and Jesus healed many who had various diseases. He also drove out many demons, but he would not let the demons speak because they knew who he was. Very early in the morning, while it was still dark, Jesus got up, left the house and went off to a solitary place, where he prayed.

Simon and his companions went to look for him, and when they found him, they exclaimed: "Everyone is looking for you!" (Mark 1:32–37)

The evening before, there had been a stupendous miracle service. The sick were healed, demons were cast out. Jesus didn't say My glory is established, I will rejoice and call all who were with Me to rejoice. After this service, Jesus did not go to bed thinking about those who had been healed. He went to bed thinking about the Father.

Good people get up in the morning at 4:00 am to meet their God.

- In the morning: 6:00 am
- Early: 5:00 am
- Very early: 4:00 am

4:00 am is the good hour. You have just woken up from sleep. The body feels rested. The tiredness is gone.

> *The Sovereign LORD has given me an instructed tongue, to know the word that sustains the weary. He wakens me morning by morning, wakens my ear to listen like one being taught. The Sovereign LORD has opened my ears, and I have not been rebellious; I have not drawn back* (Isaiah 50:4-5).

The sovereign Lord has opened my ears and I have not been rebellious. I have not drawn back to pull up my blanket again for the last lap of sleep. It is a battle and there is a choice. The spiritual life is a matter of choices. What you are today is the result of the decisions you made in the past. The choices you are making now will determine the future.

THE HIGHER PATHWAY

John Wesley lived on the same sum of money over many years in spite of enormous increase in his income, and invested the rest in the gospel.

There is a higher pathway; the pathway of sacrifice, of pommelling the body, of saying 'No' to the flesh, and so on. There is also a lower pathway which says, "I am saved, I will get to heaven even if I am the last person to enter." You may not enter at all. All salvation cost God His most precious Son. God's all demands man's all. How can I offer a lesser sacrifice when He gave His all? There is a deception that people can love Jesus and their world. That has been banned by decree number 0001 of the Presidency of Heaven. Either you go the whole way, or you do not go at all.

After the miracle service, he did not sleep and enjoy Himself. I know many nights of weeping, fear, a deep inner anguish because compared to what has been given to me, I have done too little. I know deep inner anguish, for fear that I may fail to accomplish the call of God on my life. That day, we shall lay our crowns at the feet of Jesus. Those crowns, we ought to have won will be laid at the feet of Jesus. I am afraid when I think of the soon coming of the Lord. The fear is that if there is a crown for me to win and lay at the feet of Jesus, and I fail to win that crown, then the Lord will have one crown less at His feet, and that would be terrible. Therefore, nothing at the moment comforts me. I keep crying out and I keep labouring. It is not just a matter of getting to heaven. It is a matter of winning a crown. It is a matter of all the crowns that I have to lay at His feet.

The Lord did not settle down and relax because He had performed miracles. Miracles were not on His heart. His Father was on His heart; so very early in the morning when it was still dark, Jesus woke up, withdrew to a lonely place, and prayed.

He decided that He would not see the face of man before He had seen the face of God and that He would not talk to man about God until He had talked to God about man. We have talked to man so much without response because we talk too little to God about him in prayer. When you talk to God about man, He will move man's heart so that when you talk to him, he will respond.

The Lord Jesus was not carrying out a formality. He loved His Father. Love pulls people together. He was drawn by a desire for His Father. The problem is that many believers have lost their first love. They have lost desire for Him. The fire that once burned in their hearts is out. They are satisfied without Him. The longing is no longer there.... Someone or something else has stolen their hearts.

As for Jesus, the crowds were there, but the crowds could not satisfy Him because His heart belonged exclusively to His Father. The great miracles could not satisfy Him. I am troubled by people who were once on fire for God but are no longer on fire.

> *The seed that fell among thorns stands for those who hear, but as they go on their way they are choked by life's worries, riches and pleasures, and they do not mature* (Luke 8:14).

The seed that fell among thorns was chocked by life's worries —husband, wife, relatives, children and so on.

Evaluate everything in terms of twenty francs—the cost of a tract. One phone call can cause many souls to perish.

Some of the best souls are sacrificed on the altar of worry. When the cancer called worry sets in a heart, the heart begins to decay.

Because of these, the seed does not mature. Are you still where you were five years ago, ten years ago, fifteen years ago, twenty years ago, last year? The seed is chocked!

Oh, that we may have the joy of a child, free from worries, relaxed about money, knowing that the One who feeds the ravens, will take care of us! Free from worries about finances of the work; fully convinced that God's work, done God's way, will never lack resources. An old man, long ago, told a younger one; "Let nothing worry you. Let nothing trouble you. Everything is passing away!"

In Jesus, all my needs are provided. Not your crazy luxuries. If you are not at peace with two pairs of trousers, you will not be at peace with twenty pairs. The problem is not trousers. It is a heart empty of God. Nothing else can satisfy it.

HOW JESUS PRAYED

Why did Jesus withdraw to a lonely place? Because the praying of Jesus was violent.

> During the days of Jesus' life on earth, he offered up prayers and petitions with loud cries and tears to the one who could save him from death, and he was heard because of his reverent submission (Hebrews 5:7).

Prayer, petitions, loud cries, tears to the one who could save Him. He didn't want to disturb those who were in the house. He withdrew, so that His loud cries and tears could be heard only by the Father. There are times when if you don't pray aloud you feel like breaking inside.

There is time for mourning and weeping, but there is also a time for loud cries. That is how the Lamb prayed. So He went to a lonely place. He was also waiting on God.

For God to speak there has to be a waiting soul, waiting for God. So the Lord Jesus had to wait before His Father to receive instructions for the day on how to answer those who would ask Him questions, heal the sick, and so on.

The Father gave Him the blueprint for the day, and He went into the day in full assurance. Some meet God in the evening after having given the best of the day to their desires. If you buy a car for your father, don't you take it to him when it is new? God must have the best. God must not have the leftovers of the day. This was the normal habit of Jesus.

Peter and the others found Him and said, "Everyone is looking for you." If He had not gone early, they would have trapped Him! Everyone was looking for Him; He was looking for His Father.

Will God speak to you? Is there a sin-free heart? If there is some sin, confess it and forsake it, so that God can speak to you. If there is sin, don't say, "God take it away." Say, "In the Name of Jesus, I take it away." Take the idol out of your heart. Your sin may not be big or great in front of man. But if someone misses the plane by one hour, of if he misses it by

- thirty minutes
- ten minutes
- one minute,

he will not happily say, "I missed it only by one minute."

A small sin will cause the same devastation as a great sin will. It will just separate you from God's best.

12

PRAYER AND DISHARMONIOUS MARRIAGES

*D*isharmonious marriages will hinder prayers. Some men will make long prayers but treat their wives badly! If a man doesn't treat his wife well, his prayers will be hindered.

> *Husbands, in the same way be considerate as you live with your wives, and treat them with respect as the weaker partner and as heirs with you of the gracious gift of life, so that nothing will hinder your prayers* (1 Peter 3:7).

Don't be a hypocrite. Disharmony with your wife means disharmony with God.

If there is war between you and your wife, there is war with God. Don't you see that God is not answering you because you have made life bitter for your wife? The door to God's closet is sealed to anyone who has a broken relationship with his wife.

By the time you took someone's daughter, you knew the value that she had then. What have you done to her? You have transformed her into a wreck. When she thinks of what she was and what she has become, does she sigh with deep regret that she ever said "Yes" to you?

What have you made her into? Is she a rejoicing woman or is she frustrated because of all that you have done—wicked words, wicked looks—to crush her? If your wife is not more fulfilled today than when you married her, then you have failed.

Look at your wife, she has grown cranky and ugly or fat and ugly because of your harsh treatment. If she was like what she is today, would you have married her? Can you say, "I thank God because my wife is fulfilled, I have transformed her into a woman in intimacy with God, in fulfilment with God?"

Has she discovered a better man than she thought you were in the course of living with you or is she shocked that you are a wolf in sheep clothing? Does she want to run away but for the fact that she lacks courage?

As a result of my preaching tours, I have become frightened. The marriages of many believers are breaking and it is largely because of the extreme selfishness of husbands. There is hypocrisy in the house of God. No wonder there is much noise called prayer, and so little answers. Are there answers corresponding to the praying?

There are not only suffering women. There are suffering men. It is only that men suffer and do not complain.

98% of women have sought marriage counselling compared to 2% men. The men suffer silently. The women pull them from one counsellor to another. The model for marriage has been thrown away completely.

The LORD God said, "It is not good for the man to be alone. I will make a helper suitable for him" (Genesis 2:18).

It is not good that man should be alone. Modern marriage is partnership, each with his own shares and each defends his rights.

The Lord said, "I will make a helper fit for him;" He did not say, "I will make a partner fit for him." The wife is a helper! Most women don't know this at all. They are partners. They have their rights to defend.

What does a helper mean?

Are you a helper or a rival?

Are you a partner or a helper?

God wanted a helper for the man. You were looking for a man to enter into partnership with you, so that you may have equal shares in the company. Why did you decide to marry him without settling in your heart that you wanted to help him?

How can a woman follow a man whose heart is sold to the world? How can a woman who seeks the Lord seven days a week follow a man who seeks the Lord two hours on Sunday morning?

How can a woman who wakes up at 4:00 or 5:00 to seek God follow a man who wakes up at seven expecting his breakfast? The one who is ahead is the leader.

Leadership is directly proportional to the knowledge of God. The one who permits his wife to follow God more intensely has abandoned leadership to his wife.

Consecrated men are in short supply.

Call for a prayer meeting and you will find more women there. Declare a fast and you will find more women fasting.

Ask people to give sacrificially and the trend is the same.

Brothers, what is this manhood all about? If a man cannot provide a shoulder-high gap in the pursuit of God; seeking of God, knowing of God, hatred of all sin, dying to self, separation from the things of the world, radical discipleship, prayer, fasting and giving to God, he has abandoned leadership to his wife.

Most wives are more consecrated than the men. Most men are tied to the

world. Many men are lazier than women.

This is a call for the men to abandon laziness! If you don't work harder than your wife, you have abandoned leadership. The one who is ahead by hard work, has the authority to command.

Men, will you acknowledge that you have been selfish, inconsiderate and unfair to your wives?

I told the missionaries, "If you do not want your wife to go on retreats, you will have a shallow wife." Twice a week, a woman should go on retreat and come back to make supper that is from 6:00am to 6:00pm.

We made the following decisions when I was in Benin:

1. Once a month, the husband and his wife should have an 8-hour night of prayer
2. One day a month, the husband must cook for the family.

So the wife has one day of holiday from working. The man has twenty-nine.

A man who is inconsiderate toward his wife will have his prayers hindered.

If God decides today that the men should become the women and the women the men, so that the wife does to you exactly what you have been doing to her, will you like it? From this day, I call all husbands to change in the name of Jesus, who will judge the living and the dead. In everything treat your wife as you would like to be treated.

A helper is not a slave.

> *Pray that a new thing will happen in the men, so that they become models to their wives and children.*

It is urgent for the development of a new kind of leadership.

I have daughters. The thought that some fool should treat them badly someday, goes right to my heart. I took a decision to treat my wife as I would like my daughters to be treated, like an egg; not just an egg; a cracked egg that needs to be treated more carefully.

I have changed and I command you to change.

> Pray for a revolution in men, that there be
> radical pursuit of Jesus
> radical consecration
> total consecration
> men on fire 100% for Jesus.
> men that Jesus can be proud of
> men who women can follow with total
>   confidence

> men who have radically forsaken sin
> men who are mightily anointed by the Holy
>   Spirit
> men who render total service for Him who gave
>   His life for us.

Men ought to be considerate, loving husbands of their wives so that it would be a joy for the wives to help their husbands, to be sweet, tender, loving and gentle. Some men are like the quilts of a porcupine. Each time you touch them they pierce! Their words are like swords they tear their wives into pieces!

> Pray that men would be lovable, people who
>   can be helped

Children must be brought up by both husband and wife, in the fear of the Lord. The husband is the disciplinarian to say, "This is the way!"

Some men run away from disciplining the child and may even tell their wives to leave the children alone. The husband and wife will team up together to produce children, after the heart of God in the glory of God and for a strong church.

We want powerful nations. Let us have powerful homes.

For nations to go right, homes must go right.

The wife should be the vice president and not the leader of the opposition. In some homes the opposition is so strong that the government is overthrown. Before you point a finger at your president, first look at how the presidency of your home is run.

Before you point a finger at rebels, find out whether there are rebels in your home.

The opposition in your home must be subdued.

For the nation to go well, the home must go well. For the right leadership in the nation, there must be right leadership in the homes. For right relationship to authority in the nation, there must be right relationship to authority in the home. No nation can go beyond the condition of her homes.

The home must go right. There must be a woman who treats her husband as lord. The man must come home to his empire. At the office, they knock him here and there. He must come home to reign. If you don't reign in your home, you have been knocked out.

For the nations to go right, the homes must go right.

For the home to go right, parents must go right.

> Pray that the homes represented in this conference would go right.
> Pray that the homes in this nation, by God's intervention, would go right.

When a woman marries a believer, it ought to be settled permanently that there is no

other woman in his life. When a Christian wife has to carry the pain that the crook, who says he is born again, is having an affair with another woman then we need a redefinition of the phrase "born again!"

Is your wife the only woman in your life?

Is your husband the only man in your life?

What does the God who sees in secret say?

Are you a pastor living in adultery?

Are you an elder and an adulterer?

Are you a deacon?

Are you a believer, born again but have another woman in your life? What have we believed? What have you believed?

If there is another woman in your thoughts; God has already put you aside, because God looks at the heart.

This Pentecostalism that lacks sanctification is a new kind of Pentecostalism. This is a new kind of baptism into the Holy Spirit! Which spirit is that?—The spirit that dwells in the fornicator?

There is a fresh anointing—is it an anointing to be immoral? Where is the holiness that is the central issue in the New Testament church? Are you true? Can you tell your wife: "God knows that I have been true to you?"

Can you tell your husband, "God knows that I have been there for you with my spirit soul and body?" Without this, much noise in prayer will mean nothing.

13
PRAYER AND HOLINESS

Where are the men to lift up holy hands? I fear that Christianity in Uganda is no longer what it used to be. There are large numbers, but very little quality. Are you a traitor of God? Are you a traitor of your husband?

God says, "I know you Judas!" And God calls you to repent. God calls you to repent. Now is the moment of repentance. If you have been pretending that you are born again but you have never really received the Lord Jesus, repent!

I learnt recently not to rush to pray with people. It is wise to give time

- for conviction to deepen;
- to let the ones I pray with to weigh issues in their hearts;
- to write out all sins they can remember.
- to meet those who are seriously convicted and will want to forsake all sin.
- to pray that the convicting power of Jesus would deepen.

It is a terrible thing when the church and the world are similar.

Praying Hyde was sent to India as a missionary with an older missionary. At an evangelistic meeting, the older missionary preached violently that Jesus sets free from sin. An Indian Hindu told Hyde, "I hope you too have been set free from sin as that man said." The word pierced his heart, and he knew he had to go back to America. If you are a slave to one sin, you are just like one who is a slave to all sins; you have no mandate to preach the gospel. You can only produce captives like yourself.

Has Jesus set you free from sin? If He has not you are a false messenger!

My mandate to say these things is that there is no sin in my life that I know of. If the Holy Spirit were to point out something now, I would do nothing until it is got rid of.

Jesus sets free from all sin. If He came to set free from some sins and not others, then He is not the Saviour. Is there a sin hidden in your heart? Then you have disqualified yourself. Are you harbouring one sin? Is there one clear area of falsehood that you know of, but have not forsaken? If there is then you are disqualified. Will you turn from that sin now and from all sin forever?

If Jesus has not set you free from all sin, what message do you have for the nation. Stop poisoning the nation. Tell the people, "Jesus does not set free from sin," and go back home to perish.

Is there sin in your life? It is very small. You can get rid of it but you have not done so. You ought to take a gun and shoot it, but you have spared it! It will soon kill you. God is giving a final warning to many people because of the sin in their hearts—long standing sin.

Pray that

- *the Holy Spirit who is warning some people would wait to the end and win.*
- *people would crumble by the sheer depth of their hypocrisy.*
- *God would constrain the hearts of people to repent, that God would convict some who are still keeping sin in their lives.*

Sin is forgiven when it is forsaken. The next time you commit it you may die. There are sins that lead to death.

Uzzah touched the ark and died. The man of God from Judah ate against the command of God and died. When a believer knows that this is a sin, and he commits it, he may have written off his life. When Amnon committed incest with Tamar, he wrote off his life and died for it soon afterwards. Rachel stole Laban's household gods, sat on them and said she was having her period it was a sin unto death. She died!

Nadab and Abihu–died for offering strange fires to God. Moses and Aaron struck the rock and died on the way to the Promised Land.

To knowingly commit a sin, you may not live to tell the story. You may not have the power to repent! If the sin that leads to death varies from person to person, you may say, I committed it last time and nothing happened. But the next time you commit it, it might lead to death. It is attempting suicide.

A normal believer should know a ten-fold deliverance at least from.

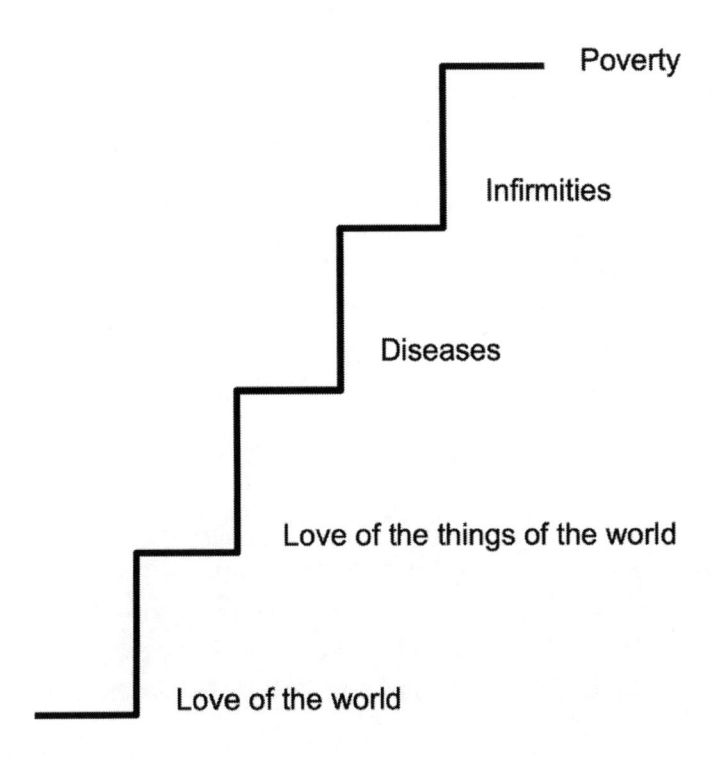

```
                                    Poverty
                            Infirmities
                   Diseases
            Love of the things of the world
    Love of the world
```

For each of the above, there is a crisis and a process.

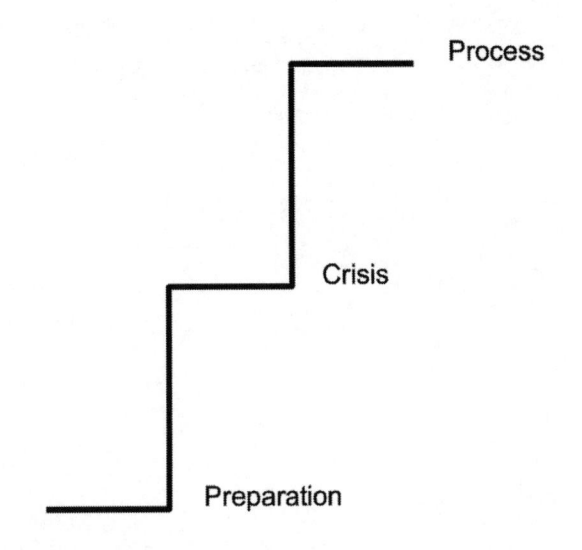

```
                          Process
                Crisis
    Preparation
```

Deliverance from hell (justification).

Time of preparation, weighing, counting the cost.

When Jesus is received, it is a crisis. It is a transfer from the kingdom of darkness into the kingdom of light, of the Son God loves.

For he has rescued us from the dominion of darkness and brought us into the kingdom of the Son he loves (Colossians 1:13).

What we call being saved or born again, is a change of kingdoms—a transfer from the kingdom of darkness to the kingdom of light, from the dominion of Satan to the dominion where Jesus is worshipped.

In the process, your eyes are opened to the depth of your sins, of how horrible you have been. Sin is a knife into God's heart. It is the recrucifixion of the Lord. All sin, however small is disastrous beyond telling. The worst thing that a man can do is to sin. When a man tells a lie or casts an immoral look, it is tragic beyond telling. When a man is hard towards his wife, wicked towards her, it is wickedness. When a man is selfish, driving his car and parking it without consideration for others, it is wickedness.

A car with a "Jesus saves" sticker on it that is driven at terrific speed is saying that God should save the man driving.

David committed adultery in secret. Amnon his son committed incest. You will see your sins exaggerated in your children.

Conversions where sin is not dealt with radically and forsaken are counterfeit conversions. George Whitefield, the great evangelist, sometimes used to lie down before God for seven days. He wrote a book about "Imitation Conversions,"—counterfeit conversions.

The counterfeit converts put on the outward form of believers. They look real, but are empty inside!

You can be a pastor, elder, or member in any kind of group but you are fake.

Confess, "I am fake, I am still lost; I want to be saved."

Counterfeit means that the outward acts are correct, but inside, you know no union with Jesus and you want God's life.

Dealing with counterfeit conversion is not a matter of one minute. There are no short cuts to dealing with sin. Deep calls for deep.

Conflicts between father and mother open the door for evil spirits to come in. Parents may be stronger and resist but the children are victims. If you want God to pour His best on your superficial treatment of sin, you are most deceived.

Romans chapter 7 describes a person who goes round in circles; sin-repent-sin-repent.

Then there comes a revelation of Christ as the Sanctifier. You can go for years without knowingly committing sin. You walk in the sanctification shield.

There must come that day when through the crisis of sanctification, you move to Romans 8. The unsanctified life is like playing football in your own goal area. The slightest mistake leads to a goal scored by the enemy's kingdom. When you are sanctified, your goal area is free.

> Pray that God gives you a long-range view of sin.

When your life is sanctified, God gives you long range vision to see the sin from afar, and tell the devil to back off.

One thing that happens in the sanctified life is that God blots out all the memories of the past. It is when people link a naked woman to the experience of the past that they begin to lust.

Even for one who was very immoral, all that past is wiped away. If the Son of God shall set you free, you shall be free indeed. It is total freedom.

You receive deliverance from hell by receiving Jesus as Saviour.

You receive deliverance from sin by receiving Jesus as the Sanctifier.

14
PRAYER AND LOVERS

When you are with someone you love you have only one enemy—time. The fact that believers pray for fifteen minutes and think that it was for one hour reveals that the church has been seduced from loving the Lord. Look at your prayer life, it is an exposure of your heart. The fact that they have to keep telling you about the need to pray is evidence of a heart disease.

Do you want to acknowledge that you don't love Jesus? Have you ever been honest before God, and said, "God, I don't love You?"

The problem with believers is that they confess lies until their hearts are hardened.

Have you ever told God; I don't spontaneously desire you; I don't spontaneously bow to You? I don't find the time with You too short.

This shows that you don't love Him.

Why don't you go back? After twenty years in the Lord, you are still a stranger to Jesus; you gasp for speech. Even at first contact lovers have a lot to say to each other.

What is this disease that has killed the people of God so that after many years they are still strangers to Jesus?

It could be because of falsehood. They say they love the word whereas they don't and because they continue to confess that, there is no opportunity for God to intervene. Why don't you own up and say, "Lord Jesus, I don't love You. I am a stranger to You. Teach me how to love You, because on my own, I have failed." The first step for anything to happen in somebody's life is stark honesty! There are husbands who ought to tell their wives, "I don't love you, I want to love you." If they are that honest, they will bring forth results.

Because people prefer lies, after many years, there is no prayer. The lord Jesus spent the night praying to God.

R.A. Torrey says most believers don't pray. They make noise, throwing things here and there! He prayed to God! Do you pray to God or you pray to yourself? The Pharisee prayed to himself,

> *The Pharisee stood up and prayed about himself: 'God, I thank you that I am not like other men—robbers, evildoers, adulterers—or even like this tax collector* (Luke 18:11).

Do you pray to yourself or you pray to God? Have you ever prayed to God? How long ago since you last prayed to God? Could it be that you stopped praying to God and now you are praying to yourself? No one who knows that there is some sin in his life, unconfessed can pray to God. When a man has a misunderstanding with his wife, the Bible says, "Keep your offering, first go and be reconciled with your neighbour."

Those who pray to God are utterly sensitive to sin. They are desperate to be correct. They labour to maintain a clear conscience before God and man. Others are bound by acrobatics; they don't care what happens, they are satisfied provided they make noise.

If there is one known sin in your life, then you have never prayed. When there is sin, you can pray to man, but you cannot pray to God. How many years have you wasted? When Abraham took Hagar and went into her, the heavens were sealed for fourteen years. How long have the heavens been sealed over you? Will you be honest and say, "The heavens have been sealed over me for years?"

For how long can you continue to go on? Have you not wasted enough time? Things have changed. You are no longer the same man or woman.

You are busy with activities but you know you are out of touch with God. Have you come to the end of yourself? How long? How long? How long?

When you pray with people, you build them up. The Lord Jesus took the disciples to the mountain to pray.

> ... *He took Peter, John and James with him and went up onto a mountain to pray. As he was praying, the appearance of his face changed, and his clothes became as bright as a flash of lightning* (Luke 9:28-29).

Nine years ago; I spent nine days praying with four brethren. Today the brother is a director of prayer; one sister is the principal of the School of Knowing and Serving God. The second sister is in charge of the School of Prayer. The place of prayer is where the training takes place. When you pray with people, they come to God. People are built in the process of praying with them.

It is not a few words uttered. It is that together you are lost in the presence of God in deep worship. People mature and are transformed in the place of prayer. If you don't pray with someone, you are not building him up.

When husband and wife don't pray together, frequently and for long, they can't be intimate with one another. Every Christian marriage that broke up, first broke up in the place of prayer. When people break from praying together, they have buried their relationship. In prayer there is union. Prayer is the place where balloons are deflated.

When you discuss things with people and you don't pray together, you accomplish nothing. Your inner circle has to have more times of prayer with you. The Lord Jesus was normal before He started praying. As He was praying, He was transfigured. The disciples almost missed everything because they were sleeping. What if Jesus had not prayed? He would not have been transfigured.

15

PRAYER AND THE RAISING OF WORKERS

After this the Lord appointed seventy-two others and sent them two by two ahead of him to every town and place where he was about to go. He told them, "The harvest is plentiful, but the workers are few. Ask the Lord of the harvest, therefore, to send out workers into his harvest field" (Luke 10:1-2).

God does this in answer to prayer. The church does everything else in order to have workers except pray. Instead of praying, we choose some people, send them to dangerous schools and give them dangerous titles and then send them out into our harvest.

The Lord asked, "Whose harvest is it?" It is His harvest, therefore, we should pray and He will send forth labourers into His harvest.

If you are the hasty type, you are dangerous because when God has not spoken, you will go running. There is nothing that tests an activist like prayer. To sit and pray for

two hours is death to him.

God gives people work and expects them to wait on Him.

"Pray ye therefore the Lord of the harvest that he might release funds into the harvest." Instead of praying to the Lord of the harvest, we send letters. This is the spirit of the world. This is the spirit of Satan. It can only destroy. We prefer to turn to man because man is nearer than God. This is most unfortunate. There is no God who is the God of the third world and another God who is the God of the first world. He is one God but the heart must be free from the love of things. He must be trusted. The manipulations of men must stop.

"Pray therefore, the Lord of the harvest." If we will not pray, there will be no labourers. If we do not pray, there will be no funds from God; we will then resort to manipulating men.

The disciples did not say, "Teach us how to preach." They could preach.

They didn't say, "Lord teach us how to heal or cast out demons." They could preach without being taught.

In the University of God, prayer is the most difficult course. Even bright students need to be taught. Prayer is that course that needs to be taught or it will not be mastered. Who is your teacher of prayer? If you don't have one, you may not know how to pray.

How many Schools of Prayer are there?

Who is the principal?

Where is the School of Fasting? Who is the principal?

Where is the Academy of Walking by Faith?

Why are these critical schools not available? You can't run a School of Fasting if you don't fast. You may deceive the first batch, but the second batch will catch you.

There are no schools because there are no teachers. There are no teachers because the lessons are courses on both life and theory.

One who is lukewarm about prayer is a spectator.

Oh, that there will be the Uganda School of Prayer and the Uganda School of Fasting! These are desperate needs.

Who has done ten forty-day fasts so that he can guide fasting people along!

Who has done five; or who has done one? When you have to advertise the posts for the School of Fasting, to qualify, the principal should have done ten forty-day fasts.

The minimum qualification for a lecturer should be at least two forty-day fasts.

Will you find the staff?

For the post of an office messenger, an applicant should have done at least one twenty-one-day fast. A chief clerk should have done at least three fasts of twenty-one days.

You will start confronting the fact that there is no staff.

For the School of Prayer, bring 2000 very obvious answers to prayer that prove that you can move God to answer prayer. Those are the kinds of qualifications that we require but where are the candidates?

The Lord is looking for people whose own lives are a school of prayer. People who move God to move men; people who are known in hell.

Jesus prayed!

16
THE PRIORITY IN PRAYER

When the disciples asked Him to teach them to pray, He taught them and began with, "Our Father"

1. <u>Priority 1:</u> "Hallowed be thy name"—the holiness of the saints at prayer before God.
2. <u>Priority 2:</u> "Thy kingdom come"—(on knees bowed) my kingdom must give away.
3. <u>Priority 3:</u> "Thy will be done."

These are all the three priorities in prayer. All the other things are secondary. Prayer is firstly centred around imposing the glory of God, secondly His kingdom and thirdly His will.

Are you caught up with the holiness of God's name? Are you caught up with the will of God? Or is it your head, leg, in-laws, cat, dog and so on that you are caught up with?

If the three priorities are not your priorities, then you are mistaken.

If you are preoccupied with praying for His Kingdom, He will take care of your own

kingdom.

There is a living God who asked His people to pray from a position of holiness, and He will answer. He does answer. When in heaven, we will see what we missed; our one regret will be, why we prayed so little.

I want to labour to make progress in prayer. I invite you to make progress in prayer.

The question is, "What have I accomplished in my locality?" You cannot build a work on students. They are there but very soon they will not be available. You cannot build a work on a shifting population if you want to succeed. You cannot build a work on girls who are waiting to be married. Tomorrow somebody will come and take them away. You cannot build a work on wives of people who are not in the assembly; committed as they are, when their husbands smash their heads, they may become secret disciples whom you will be unable to count on.

When you have a family head, you have begun the work. You can also count on a sister who is not planning to get married; She is looking for God, not a man to come and deliver her from loneliness. You go for a family head.

You go for family heads. It's not that you turn your back to the others, but you build on family heads. When a family head decides to follow the Lord, he is settled. Children could be lower down. During holidays they are away.

If I meet somebody on the road, I will tell him the gospel, but if I want to evangelize, I will not go to the road. That is lazy evangelism. A man can lock his wife and children within. But no woman can lock the man within. He will look for a way out.

In church planting, you go for family heads. You just don't go into the streets that's lousy evangelism. You go to homes; from house to house.

When I don't see family heads in the church, I know it is still a joke.

If I am to go for women, I will go for mature women not young girls still under their

Parents' authority. You can go on for years but until you have family heads you will not have a stable work. You can have wives who sneak to meetings. They have their place in the assembly but they cannot be building blocks.

The first building block should be a man.

The second should be a man and his wife.

The third building block should be a mature woman who is single and can decide for herself.

Family heads in a church make solid churches. The advantage is that parents will help in discipling their children. It is not you who shall become Mr. disciple-maker-general who disciples from the two-year-old to the grandfather.

Missionaries are not desperate for souls otherwise there would be evangelism every night! If you spend three to four hours every day in evangelism, you will have souls. Anything less than that is utter laziness.

A person who makes much efforts, then stops, waits for some time, then makes efforts cannot make much progress.

Why can you not witness three to four hours every day for one year? Tell me that you put in 1000 hours of evangelism in one year... but if you can go on without results, you will go on. If you can go on with little results, you will. There is the human factor in God's work.

There were many apostles. Why is it that Paul wrote many books in the New Testament? It is the human factor in God's work.

When a missionary couple is not in deep harmony, God stays out. When the wife pulls the man away from the work to the problems generated by her self-centredness, it cannot work. When something is lacking in the man's consecration, it will not work. If the man is consecrated and the wife is not, it will not work because we sent out two, not one. When you look at the joint prayer input of the man and his wife and find the average, ask if that average can break into new grounds. Consecration demands that you take the average and ask if you can break new grounds.

The devil only yields grounds that he can no longer keep when he is evicted—forced out!

A brother who was getting numbers was fasting three days complete a week. Then the numbers got to 102. When he stopped fasting, it dropped to 70. Statistics show that everything is tied to what is happening in the spiritual.

One quarrel with your wife may cost you the harvest.

If you pay the price, and use the wrong method, it will not work; for example, evangelizing at bus stops.

Everything depends on the price paid. If you are praying three hours a day and things are not happening, increase to four hours a day, then to five hours a day. You have to force things to happen.

The evangelist has no time for counselling people; he doesn't settle, rather, he goes from one place to another. To settle is to say that you are idle.

People should go and tell their problems to their pastors and not to the evangelist. It is time stolen from evangelism. I will not counsel a woman without her husband.

Is it fair to choose a pastor, yet when you have a problem, you go to another person?

In fact, you are confusing the person and subverting the other pastor. If it is the pastor that brings the person's problem to you, you can help them. Otherwise, when you're counselling him, you don't know what he has heard before from other counsellors.

Keep to your flock! Keep to your flock!

BACK MATTERS

VERY IMPORTANT!!!

If you have not yet received Jesus as your Lord and Saviour, I encourage you to receive Him. Here are some steps to help you,

ADMIT that you are a sinner by nature and by practice and that on your own you are without hope. Tell God you have personally sinned against Him in your thoughts, words and deeds. Confess your sins to Him, one after another in a sincere prayer. Do not leave out any sins that you can remember. Truly turn from your sinful ways and abandon them. If you stole, steal no more. If you have been committing adultery or fornication, stop it. God will not forgive you if you have no desire to stop sinning in all areas of your life, but if you are sincere, He will give you the power to stop sinning.

BELIEVE that Jesus Christ, who is God's Son, is the only Way, the only Truth and the only Life. Jesus said,

> "*I am the way, the truth and the life; no one comes to the Father, but by me*" (*John 14:6*).

The Bible says,

> "For there is one God, and there is one mediator between God and men, the man Christ Jesus, who gave himself as a ransom for all" (1 Timothy 2:5-6).

> "And there is salvation in no one else (apart from Jesus), for there is no other name under heaven given among men by which we must be saved" (Acts 4:12).

> But to all who received him, who believed in his name, he gave power to become children of God..." (John 1:12).

BUT,

CONSIDER the cost of following Him. Jesus said that all who follow Him must deny themselves, and this includes selfish financial, social and other interests. He also wants His followers to take up their crosses and follow Him. Are you prepared to abandon your own interests daily for those of Christ? Are you prepared to be led in a new direction by Him? Are you prepared to suffer for Him and die for Him if need be? Jesus will have nothing to do with half-hearted people. His demands are total. He will only receive and forgive those who are prepared to follow Him AT ANY COST. Think about it and count the cost. If you are prepared to follow Him, come what may, then there is something to do.

INVITE Jesus to come into your heart and life. He says,

> "Behold I stand at the door and knock. If anyone hears my voice and opens the door (to his heart and life), I will come in to him and eat with him, and he with me " (Revelation 3:20).

Why don't you pray a prayer like the following one or one of your own construction as the Holy Spirit leads?

> "Lord Jesus, I am a wretched, lost sinner who has sinned in thought, word and deed. Forgive all my sins and cleanse me. Receive me, Saviour and transform me into a child of God. Come into my heart now and give me eternal life right now. I will follow you at all costs, trusting the Holy Spirit to give me all the power I need."

When you pray this prayer sincerely, Jesus answers at once and justifies you before God and makes you His child.

*Please write to us (**ztfbooks@cmfionline.org**) and I will pray for you and help you as you go on with Jesus Christ.*

THANK YOU

For Reading This Book

If you have any question and/or need help, do not hesitate to contact us through zftbooks@cmfionline.org. If the book has blessed you, then we would also be grateful if you leave a positive review at your favorite retailer.

ZTF BOOKS, through Christian Publishing House (CPH) offers a wide selection of best selling Christian books (in print, eBook & audiobook formats) on a broad spectrum of topics, including marriage & family, sexuality, practical spiritual warfare, Christian service, Christian leadership, and much more. Visit us at ztfbooks.com to learn more about our latest releases and special offers. And thank you for being a ZTF BOOK reader.

We invite you to connect with more from the author through social media (cmfionline) and/or ministry website (ztfministry.org), where we offer both on-ground and remote training courses (all year round) from basic to university level at the University of Prayer and Fasting (WUPF) and the School of Knowing and Serving God (SKSG). You are highly welcome to enrol at your soonest convenience. A FREE online Bible Course is also available.

We would like to recommend to you another suitable book in **This Series** - *Practical Spiritual Warfare Through Prayer*:

In this handbook, *Professor Fomum* demonstrates, in very powerful terms, the

determinant role of prayer in spiritual warfare.

The burden he is labouring to discharge is to <u>bring every believer to develop an ever-increasing life of prayer</u>, with the aim of destroying the devil's plans and purposes. Throughout his message, it emerges that to wage spiritual warfare, you must:

1. Identify your enemy;
2. Build a hedge of protection around you and around everything that belongs to you. That should be in addition to the hedge already built by God.
3. For more range in combat, you've got to draft in a great number of people of quality;
4. You and them have got to be united for the same purpose;
5. Do not omit **the role of angels in combat**.
6. Finally, know that whoever engages in combat must persevere until the end. Don't ever give up till victory.

This book is **a very practical and precious work** meant to lead you to realise, as a believer, that you must pray or perish.

Read it now and act!

ABOUT THE AUTHOR

Professor Zacharias Tanee Fomum was born in the flesh on 20th June 1945 and became born again on 13th June 1956. On 1st October 1966, He consecrated his life to the Lord Jesus and to His service, and was filled with the Holy Spirit on 24th October 1970. He was taken to be with the Lord on 14th March, 2009.

Pr Fomum was admitted to a first class in the Bachelor of Science degree, graduating as a prize winning student from Fourah Bay College in the University of Sierra Leone in October 1969. At the age of 28, he was awarded a Ph.D. in Organic Chemistry by the University of Makerere, Kampala in Uganda. In October 2005, he was awarded a Doctor of Science (D.Sc) by the University of Durham, Great Britain. This higher doctorate was in recognition of his distinct contributions to scientific knowledge through research. As a Professor of Organic Chemistry in the University of Yaoundé 1, Cameroon, Professor Fomum supervised or co-supervised more than 100 Master's Degree and Doctoral Degree theses and co-authored over 160 scientific articles in leading international journals. He considered Jesus Christ the Lord of Science ("For by Him all things were created..." – Colossians 1:16), and scientific research an act of obedience to God's command to "subdue the earth" (Genesis 1:28). He therefore made the Lord Jesus the Director of his research laboratory while he took the place of deputy director, and attributed his outstanding success as a scientist to Jesus' revelational leadership.

In more than 40 years of Christian ministry, Pr Fomum travelled extensively, preaching the Gospel, planting churches and training spiritual leaders. He made more than:

- 700 missionary journeys within Cameroon, which ranged from one day to three weeks in duration.
- 500 missionary journeys to more than 70 different nations in all the six continents. These ranged from two days to six weeks in duration.

By the time of his going to be with the Lord in 2009, he had preached in over 1000 localities in Cameroon, sent over 200 national missionaries into many localities in Cameroon and planted over 1300 churches in the various administrative provinces of Cameroon. At his base in Yaoundé, he planted and built a mega-church with his co-workers which grew to a steady membership of about 12,000. Pr Fomum was the founding team-leader of Christian Missionary Fellowship International (CMFI); an evangelism, soul-winning, disciple making, Church-planting and missionary-sending movement with more than 200 international missionaries and thousands of churches in 65 nations spread across Africa, Europe, the Americas, Asia and Oceania. In the course of their ministry, Pr Fomum and his team witnessed more than 10,000 recorded healing miracles performed by God in answer to prayer in the name of Jesus Christ. These miracles include instant healings of headaches, cancers, HIV/AIDS, blindness, deafness, dumbness, paralysis, madness, and new teeth and organs received.

Pr Fomum read the entire Bible more than 60 times, read more than 1350 books on the Christian faith and authored over 150 books to advance the Gospel of Jesus Christ. 5 million copies of these books are in circulation in 12 languages as well as 16 million gospel tracts in 17 languages.

Pr Fomum was a man who sought God. He spent between 15 minutes and six hours daily alone with God in what he called Daily Dynamic Encounters with God (DDEWG). During these DDEWG he read God's Word, meditated on it, listened to God's voice, heard God speak to him, recorded what God was saying to him and prayed it through. He thus had over 18,000 DDEWG. He also had over 60 periods of withdrawing to seek God alone for periods that ranged from 3 to 21 days (which he termed Retreats for Spiritual Progress). The time he spent seeking God slowly transformed him into a man who hungered, thirsted and panted after God. His unceasing heart cry was: "Oh, that I would have more of God!"

Pr Fomum was a man of prayer and a leading teacher on prayer in many churches and conferences around the world. He considered prayer to be the most important work that can be done for God and for man. He was a man of faith who believed that God answers prayer. He kept a record of his prayer requests and had over 50, 000 recorded answers to prayer in his prayer books. He carried out over 100 Prayer Walks of between five and forty-seven kilometres in towns and cities around the world. He and his team carried out over 57 Prayer Crusades (periods of forty days and nights during which at least eight hours are invested into prayer each day). They also carried out over 80 Prayer Sieges (times of near non-stop praying that ranges from 24 hours to 120 hours). He authored the Prayer Power Series, a 13-volume set of books on various aspects of prayer; Supplication, Fasting, Intercession and Spiritual Warfare. He started prayer chains, prayer rooms, prayer houses, national and continental prayer movements in Cameroon and other nations. He worked with leaders of local churches in India to disciple and train more than 2 million believers.

Pr Fomum also considered fasting as one of the weapons of Christian Spiritual Warfare. He carried out over 250 fasts ranging from three days to forty days, drinking only water or water supplemented with soluble vitamins. Called by the Lord to a distinct ministry of intercession, he pioneered fasting and prayer movements and led in battles against principalities and powers obstructing the progress of the Gospel and God's global purposes. He was enabled to carry out 3 supra – long fasts of between 52 and 70 days in his final years.

Pr Fomum chose a lifestyle of simplicity and "self- imposed poverty" in order to invest more funds into the critical work of evangelism, soul winning, church-planting and the building up of believers. Knowing the importance of money and its role in the battle to reach those without Christ with the glorious Gospel, he and his wife grew to investing 92.5% of their earned income from all sources (salaries, allowances, royalties and cash gifts) into the Gospel. They invested with the hope that, as they grew in the knowledge and the love of the Lord, and the perishing souls of people, they would one day invest 99% of their income into the Gospel.

He was married to Prisca Zei Fomum and they had seven children who are all involved in the work of the Gospel, some serving as missionaries. Prisca is a national and international minister, specializing in the winning and discipling of children to Jesus Christ. She also communicates and imparts the vision of ministry to children with a view to raising and building up ministers to them.

The Professor owed all that he was and all that God had done through him, to the unmerited favour and blessing of God and to his worldwide army of friends and co-workers. He considered himself nothing without them and the blessing of God; and would have amounted to nothing but for them. All praise and glory to Jesus Christ!

- facebook.com/cmfionline
- twitter.com/cmfionline
- instagram.com/cmfionline
- pinterest.com/cmfionline
- youtube.com/cmfionline

RECOMMENDED BOOKS

https://ztfbooks.com

THE CHRISTIAN WAY

1. The Way Of Life
2. The Way Of Obedience
3. The Way Of Discipleship
4. The Way Of Sanctification
5. The Way Of Christian Character
6. The Way Of Spiritual Power
7. The Way Of Christian Service
8. The Way Of Spiritual Warfare
9. The Way Of Suffering For Christ
10. The Way Of Victorious Praying
11. The Way Of Overcomers
12. The Way Of Spiritual Encouragement
13. The Way Of Loving The Lord

THE PRAYER POWER SERIES

1. The Way Of Victorious Praying
2. The Ministry Of Fasting
3. The Art Of Intercession
4. The Practice Of Intercession
5. Praying With Power
6. Practical Spiritual Warfare Through Prayer
7. Moving God Through Prayer
8. The Ministry Of Praise And Thanksgiving
9. Waiting On The Lord In Prayer

10. The Ministry Of Supplication
11. Life-Changing Thoughts On Prayer (Vol. 1)
12. The Centrality of Prayer
13. Life-Changing Thoughts On Prayer (Vol. 2)
14. Prayer and Spiritual Intimacy
15. Life-Changing Thoughts on Prayer (Vol. 3)
16. The Art of Worship
17. Life-Changing Thoughts on Prayer (Vol. 4)
18. Life-Changing Thoughts on Prayer (Vol. 5)
19. Learning to Importune in Prayer
20. Prayer And A Walk With God
21. From His Prayer files
22. Prayer and Holiness
23. Practical Helps in Fasting Long Fasts
24. Life-Changing Thoughts on Fasting (Vol 1)
25. Life-Changing Thoughts on Fasting (Vol 2)
26. Pray Without Ceasing
27. Pray or Perish

PRACTICAL HELPS FOR OVERCOMERS

1. Discipleship at any cost
2. The Use Of Time
3. Retreats For Spiritual Progress
4. Personal Spiritual Revival
5. Daily Dynamic Encounters With God
6. The School Of Truth
7. How To Succeed In The Christian Life
8. The Christian And Money
9. Deliverance From The Sin Of Laziness
10. The Art Of Working Hard
11. Knowing God - The Greatest Need Of The Hour

12. Restitution - An Important Message For The Overcomers
13. Revelation: A Must
14. The Overcomer As A Servant Of Man
15. True Repentance
16. You Can Receive A Pure Heart Today
17. You Can Lead Someone To The Lord Jesus Today
18. You Can Receive The Baptism Into The Holy Spirit Now
19. The Dignity Of Manual Labour
20. You Have A Talent!
21. The Making Of Disciples
22. The Secret Of Spiritual Fruitfulness
23. Are You Still A Disciple Of The Lord Jesus?
24. Who Is Truly a Disciple of The Lord Jesus?

LEADING GOD'S PEOPLE

1. Vision, Burden, Action
2. Knowing The God Of Unparalleled Goodness
3. Brokenness: The Secret Of Spiritual Overflow
4. The Secret Of Spiritual Rest
5. Spiritual Aggressiveness
6. The Character And The Personality of The Leader
7. Leading A Local Church
8. The Leader And His God
9. Revolutionary Thoughts On Spiritual Leadership
10. Leading God's People
11. Laws Of Spiritual Leadership
12. Laws Of Spiritual Success, Volume 1
13. The Shepherd And The Flock
14. Basic Christian Leadership
15. A Missionary life and a missionary heart

16. Spiritual Nobility
17. Spiritual Leadership in the Pattern of David
18. The Heart Surgery for the Potential Minister of the Gospel
19. Prerequisites For Spiritual Ministry
20. Power For Service
21. In The Crucible For Service
22. Qualifications For Serving in The Gospel
23. You, Your Team, And Your Ministry
24. Church Planting Strategies
25. Critical Ingredients for Successful Spiritual Leadership
26. The Power of a Man's All

GOD, SEX AND YOU

1. Enjoying The Premarital Life
2. Enjoying The Choice Of Your Marriage Partner
3. Enjoying The Married Life
4. Divorce And Remarriage
5. A Successful Marriage; The Husband's Making
6. A Successful Marriage; The Wife's Making
7. Life-changing Thoughts On Marriage

OFF-SERIES

1. Inner Healing
2. No Failure Needs To Be Final
3. Facing Life's Problems Victoriously
4. A Word To The Students
5. Blessings and Curses
6. Spiritual Fragrance (Volume 1)
7. Roots And Destinies

8. Walking With God (Vol. 1)
9. God Centredness
10. Victorious Dispositions
11. The Processes Of Faith
12. The Spirit-Filled Life
13. God, Money, And You
14. Knowing God And Walking With Him
15. Knowing and Serving God (Volume 2)
16. Esther
17. The Church: Rights And Responsibilities of The Believer
18. Children in God's Eternal Purposes

PRACTICAL HELPS IN SANCTIFICATION

1. Deliverance From Sin
2. The Way Of Sanctification
3. Sanctified And Consecrated For Spiritual Ministry
4. The Sower, The Seed, And The Hearts Of Men
5. Freedom From The Sin Of Adultery And Fornication
6. The Sin Before You May Lead To Immediate Death: Do Not Commit It!
7. Be Filled With The Holy Spirit
8. The Power Of The Holy Spirit In The Winning Of The Lost
9. Deliverance from the Sin of Gluttony
10. A Vessel of Honour
11. The Believer's Conscience
12. Practical Dying To Self And
13. The Spirit-filled Life
14. Issues of The Heart
15. Rebellion

MAKING SPIRITUAL PROGRESS

1. The Ministers And The Ministry of The New Covenant
2. The Cross In The Life And Ministry Of The Believer
3. Making Spiritual Progress, Volume 1
4. Making Spiritual Progress, Volume 2
5. Making Spiritual Progress, Volume 3
6. Making Spiritual Progress, Volume 4
7. Moving on With The Lord Jesus Christ
8. The Narrow Way (Volume 1)
9. Making Spiritual Progress (Volumes 1-4)

EVANGELISM

1. 36 Reasons For Winning The Lost To Christ
2. Soul Winning, Volume 1
3. Soul Winning, Volume 2
4. The Winning of The Lost as Life's Supreme Task
5. Salvation And Soul-Winning
6. Soul Winning And The Making Of Disciples
7. <u>Victorious Soul-Winning</u>

GOD LOVES YOU

1. God's Love And Forgiveness
2. The Way Of Life
3. Come Back Home My Son; I Still Love You
4. Jesus Loves You And Wants To Heal You
5. Come And See; Jesus Has Not Changed!
6. Celebrity A Mask
7. Encounter The Saviour

8. Meet The Liberator
9. Jesus Saves And Heals Today
10. Jesus is The Answer

WOMEN OF THE GLORY

1. The Secluded Worshipper: Prophetess Anna
2. Unending Intimacy: Mary of Bethany
3. Winning Love: Mary Magdalene

ZTF COMPLETE WORKS

1. The School of Soul Winners and Soul Winning
2. The Complete Works of Z.T.F on Holiness (Volume 1)
3. The Complete Works of Z.T.F on Basic Christian Doctrine
4. The Complete Works of Z.T.F on Marriage (Volume 1)
5. The Complete Works of Z.T.F on The Gospel Message (Volume 1)
6. The Complete Works of Z.T.F on Prayer (Volume 1)
7. The Complete Works of Z.T.F on Prayer (Volume 2)
8. The Complete Works of Z.T.F on Prayer (Volume 3)
9. The Complete Works of Z.T.F on Prayer (Volume 4)
10. The Complete Works of Z.T.F on Prayer (Volume 5)
11. The Complete Works of Z.T.F on Leadership (Volume 1)
12. The Complete Works of Z.T.F on Leadership (Volume 2)
13. The Complete Works of Z.T.F on Leadership (Volume 3)

SPECIAL SERIES

1. A Broken Vessel
2. The Joy of Begging to Belong to the Lord Jesus Christ: A Testimony
3. Separation from the common

ZTF AUTO-BIOGRAPHIES

1. From His Lips: About The Author
2. From His Lips: About His Co-Workers
3. From His Lips: Back From His Missions
4. From His Lips: About Our Ministry
5. From His Lips: On Our Vision
6. From His Lips: The work is the worker
7. From His Lips: The Battles He Fought
8. From His Lips: The Authority And Power of His Life
9. From His Lips: The Influences That Moulded Him: People And Books

THE OVERTHROW OF PRINCIPALITIES

1. Deliverance From Demons
2. The Prophecy Of The Overthrow Of The Satanic Prince Of Cameroon
3. The Prophecy of the Overthrow of The Satanic Prince of Yaounde
4. The Prophecy of the Overthrow of The Satanic Prince of Douala
5. The overthrow of principalities and powers
6. From His Lips: The Battles He Fought

CONTINUOUS PERSONAL SPIRITUAL REVIVAL

1. Victorious Proclamations

OTHER BOOKS

1. The Missionary as a Son
2. What Our Ministry is
3. Conserver la Moisson
4. Disciples of Jesus Christ to Make Disciples For Jesus Christ
5. The House Church in God's Eternal Purposes
6. Christian Maturation
7. Heroes of the Kingdom
8. Spiritual Leadership in the Pattern of Gideon
9. The School of Evangelism
10. A Good Minister of Jesus Christ
11. Building a Spiritual Nation: The Foundation
12. Building a Spiritual Nation: Spiritual Statesmanship
13. Removing Obstacles Through Prayer and Fasting
14. The Chronicles of Our Ministry
15. The Making of Disciples: The Master's Way
16. Watching in Prayer

DISTRIBUTORS OF ZTF BOOKS

These books can be obtained in French and English Language from any of the following distribution outlets:

EDITIONS DU LIVRE CHRETIEN (ELC)

- **Location:** Paris, France
- **Email:** editionlivrechretien@gmail.com
- **Phone:** +33 6 98 00 90 47

INTERNET

- **Location:** on all major online **eBook, Audiobook** and **print-on-demand** (paperback) retailers.
- **Email**: ztfbooks@cmfionline.org
- **Phone**: +47 454 12 804
- **Website**: ztfbooks.com

CPH YAOUNDE

- **Location:** Yaounde, Cameroon
- **Email:** editionsztf@gmail.com
- **Phone:** +237 74756559

ZTF LITERATURE AND MEDIA HOUSE

- **Location:** Lagos, Nigeria
- **Email:** zlmh@ztfministry.org
- **Phone:** +2348152163063

CPH BURUNDI

- **Location:** Bujumbura, Burundi
- **Email:** cph-burundi@ztfministry.org
- **Phone:** +257 79 97 72 75

CPH UGANDA

- **Location:** Kampala, Uganda
- **Email:** cph-uganda@ztfministry.org
- **Phone:** +256 785 619613

CPH SOUTH AFRICA

- **Location:** Johannesburg, RSA
- **Email:** tantohtantoh@yahoo.com
- **Phone**: +27 83 744 5682

Made in the USA
Columbia, SC
21 April 2023

b0307616-14d1-4e6b-acfd-c58824ca9edbR01